PROTECTING YOUR BUSINESS SECRETS

PROTECTING YOUR BUSINESS SECRETS

Michael Saunders

NP

NICHOLS PUBLISHING COMPANY : NEW YORK

First published in the United States of America in 1985 by
Nichols Publishing Company
Post Office Box 96
New York, N.Y. 10024

Printed in Great Britain

Library of Congress Cataloging in Publication Data

Saunders, Michael
  Protecting your business secrets.

  Includes index.
  1. Trade secrets 2. Business intelligence.
I. Title
HD38.7.S28 1985b   658.4'72   84-25392
ISBN 0-89397-209-6

Contents

Preface

The modern businessman is a prudent soul. He is concerned with budgeting and financial controls, makes careful plans to ensure expansion and has contingency plans to deal with the unexpected. He also has a defensive strategy, accepting the need for 'security'. Some 'security' is dictated by legislation: for example, compliance with fire regulations and Factories Acts, or providing a safe environment for employees.

Why then do so many employers who insist on locks on doors and windows to prevent thieves from stealing omit to provide defences against the more sophisticated thieves whose objectives are undoubtedly worth many times more than would interest a common burglar? Industrial and commercial spies are an ever-growing breed of sophisticated 'burglars', all the more dangerous because their activities do not necessarily involve the breaking and entering of premises usually associated with a common burglar.

Add to this the rapidly increasing range and availability of technological aid to the industrial spy, the monetary rewards for success, the lack of expertise to prevent or detect it, together with the paucity of legislation under which to prosecute it, and the net result is a growth industry of alarming proportions.

There is an element of fashion in crime, and it seems that the stealing of business secrets is regarded nowadays as more fashionable than other forms of theft requiring force or violence against persons or property.

In much the same way company fraud and manipulation are considered more fashionable than theft or robbery, with greater potential financial rewards and less risk of detection or apprehension.

Why, therefore, should so many businessmen leave themselves in a situation where they are likely to become the victims of successful attempts to steal their business secrets?

Why should their only response to such threats or attacks be reactive and not effectively pre-planned, as other business operations are? Industrial espionage is a reality. It is happening on an increasing scale and it is folly to assume that it is only directed against multinational corporations with massive contracts. Every business and type of organisation has rivals, both nationally and internationally. Everyone's livelihood is affected by those who seek an unfair advantage and will stop at nothing to gain their ends.

The need for this book is created not only by the paucity of reference to those who have suffered (largely through their reluctance to allow the particulars to be publicised), but also by the lack of information and expertise on the subject. My objective in Part I is to describe the vulnerabilities, techniques, people, situations and opportunities that should give cause for alarm. Part II seeks to indicate the areas where protection can be achieved by systematic planning.

The book is directed primarily at business managers since it is they who have both the responsibility and the authority to shape the future of their organisations. Security practitioners will also benefit from it since countering any threat to the company's profitability — or even its continued existence — is obviously a major part of their function.

It is unfortunate that films and television programmes lend a false glamour to the business of espionage. The antics of some fictional investigators together with the image created by James Bond tend to detract from the seriousness of the matter. The reality is more mundane and what really happens in the business world, how and why, makes far less sensational reading. I have attempted to portray the ungarnished facts as they are today.

I should like to thank, in alphabetical order not necessarily indicative of the value of their assistance, Alexander Autote, Derek Gilmour, Thomas Norton, Colleen O'Boyle and Dick Youd, for the help they provided with certain aspects of the book, which would not have been possible without the assistance, guidance and commitment of Malcolm Stern, my editor at Gower.

I am also grateful for the inspiration that the solitude and tranquillity of Radwinter, in the heart of the Essex countryside, has provided and the comfort and understanding of those friends and relatives who well know who they are.

Michael Saunders

Part I
Cause for Alarm

1 The Nature of Business Espionage

The outcome of world wars was influenced by it; the current conflict between West and East is affected by it; the economic survival of a nation could be determined by it; and ultimately the success or failure of one company competing against others in the same industry can depend upon it. What the military refer to as 'intelligence' or 'espionage' becomes, in a business context, research and development, market research and marketing strategy.

The Guinness Book of Records credits industrial espionage with arguably the greatest robbery of all times. Some $24m (then £8.57m) worth of papers and vials of micro-organisms − the property of the American Cyanamid Corporation and the result of years of research and development − was lost to an Italian-organised team of specialists through industrial espionage. Against such a sum of money, other entries in that book, including some notable robberies and frauds of recent times, pale into insignificance.

Technology as the target

Facts demonstrating the importance of international espionage are not hard to find. It is well known, for example, that the ability of the British Secret Service to crack German cipher systems greatly influenced the outcome of the Second World War. However, espionage is not exclusively a war-time phenomenon. At the end of the nineteenth century the Cheshire silk industry 'fell' to the Japanese, who copied its technology and, with cheaper labour and poorer working conditions, produced similar goods at much lower costs. Today, the far greater incentives and rewards of a whole new technology motivate individuals to participate in what nowadays carries the title of 'espionage'.

The Soviet Union currently exploits, through trade and cultural delegations, the opportunity to gain Western technology and techniques, East and West Germany having become the 'clearing house' for the acquisition and dissemination of the information. In the USA alone in 1974 there were 10,600 'cultural and commercial visitors' from Soviet-block countries. Between 1962 and 1965 Soviet 'diplomats' in West Germany were involved in the acquisition of numerous British, German and American documents relating to highly specialised research subjects in laser techniques and plasma physics. Since all Soviet industry is nationalised, it is logical that the State should carry out all espionage, including industrial espionage − a classic example being the Concorde/Conkordski aircraft design. However, it is in the West that we have seen what is probably the most significant recent example of espionage: the Watergate affair, which led to the downfall of Richard Nixon, former President of the United States, and the prosecution of his chief government advisers.

The East-West power struggle

We must hope that the threat of mutual nuclear destruction will prevent the great powers of East and

West engaging each other in direct military conflict, but in economic terms it could be said that a state of war exists today and will continue to be fought in the areas of commerce and industry. Thus it is that the wars of today and tomorrow are likely to be entirely economic. Nations will become or remain strong by virtue of the standing of their currency in world markets and the success of their commerce and industry compared with that of their adversaries. Britain no longer seeks her future leaders among those passing out at Dartmouth, Cranwell and Sandhurst, but rather among university science graduates and the products of the London and Manchester Business Schools. Just as individual companies may be unscrupulous in their attempts to undermine the opposition, so nations use all kinds of methods in their struggle for supremacy. The whole 'perimeter fence' of West Germany is bristling with electronic ears and eyes pointing towards the East and, from what can be seen through telescopes provided for the public at Torfhaus in the Herz mountains, the East Germans have the same sort of equipment pointing westwards.

Every force, to remain controllable, must have a counterbalance. Intelligence and espionage require counter-intelligence and counter-espionage. One force may be seen as offensive, the other defensive. America learned the dangers of an information-gathering intelligence organisation being allowed executive power when the CIA mounted the ill-starred 'Bay of Pigs' venture against Cuba. In Great Britain the police (usually the Special Branch) perform the operational tasks and action the needs of the Security Service, thus providing the counter-balance necessary to ensure control and effectiveness. It is a principle of intelligence that those whose responsibility it is to collect, collate and disseminate the information must not be responsible for acting on it. Persons charged with the latter responsibility need not only operational competence but also sound political or military judgement.

Scientifically-based espionage

Computers are playing an ever-increasing role in everyone's daily lives. Their technology has advanced to the extent that 'intelligence banks' containing all sorts of information can take only a few seconds to yield data which would previously have required immense space for storage and an enormous amount of time to retrieve. Marketing data, customers' names and addresses, credit worthiness, state of account, types and levels of discounts, payroll details, Criminal Record Office details and a whole host of other data relating to persons, companies, industries and countries can now be stored in such a way that accurate and speedy retrieval is available virtually at the touch of a button.

The ease and speed with which information can be extracted from computers makes them very vulnerable to misuse − especially when the information is extremely sensitive or when its preservation is vital to its owner. Thieves operating in the world of computers present a formidable threat to information and security. Yesterday's thief had to be skilled in breaking and entering premises, stealing and photographing files of papers or planting eavesdropping equipment; tomorrow's industrial spy may have the skills of a computer technician to obtain unlawful access to the machine or its memory store; he may obtain the assistance of experts from within the system he is trying to penetrate in order to extract (share but not steal!) any information he requires, in seconds. The risk of detection is comparatively low, and there is a paucity of legislation to deal with any offender who is caught.

It is dangerous to assume of any business that it has no secrets worth protecting. Industrial espionage, increasingly facilitated by advanced technology, is growing. The tragedy is that those who discover they have been victims are reluctant to admit it and the more successful penetrations are never revealed except on the balance sheet or, even worse, by the liquidation of the company.

The nature of the threat

Commercial organisations which are likely to be the targets of industrial espionage are vulnerable not only to spying threats from within or without but also to injury by accidental or deliberate acts just as damaging as espionage.

Prudent steps taken to minimise one kind of risk will almost certainly reduce other kinds as well. The collective defences against damage and harm will always tend to reduce the opportunities, incentives, scope for concealment and realisation of the threats to which most commercial organisations are susceptible. Those four ingredients are invariably to be found in all types of fraud. Elimination or reduction of any of them will reduce the likelihood of its happening and/or increase the possibility of its being detected before its result is critical.

Planning a defence against industrial espionage is no different from planning any other security defence. It is, after all, a security threat and physical counter-measures are just as important as functional or security systems. It makes little commercial sense to spend a fortune on physical security for a store within premises containing precious metals and neglect the security of the boardroom, computer centre or any other area where the information is generated upon which the whole future of the organisation depends.

'Secrets' at risk are not only the obvious ones such as research and development results, marketing strategies or new product launches, etc. A rival organisation may be interested in something which is so taken for granted in the company that the owner believes it has no outside value — for example, lists of customers or pricing structure. Complacency of this type is dangerous.

Proprietary information is often stolen not by trained industrial spies employing the latest electronic gadgetry but by 'amateurs' — often employees — using simple, easily available techniques, as described in the next chapter. Espionage can take many forms: discreet incursions into vulnerable areas of an organisation, with subsequent photocopying or photographing of sensitive materials; crude break-ins and outright theft of materials; or the 'buying' of a member of staff who holds valuable information. The nature of the risks facing an organisation depends largely on the scope and scale of its materials, the type of business involved, its size and success and, especially, the type of competition it faces.

Symptoms of espionage

Symptoms of successful penetrations are usually apparent to the victims. But they may not be obviously attributable to industrial espionage. People will usually find numerous reasons to justify or excuse a failure or business disappointment before accepting that industrial espionage could be the cause. How many times must a sales executive just lose out to the same competitor on a carefully drawn sealed bid tender before he suspects some 'unfair' practice? How many times must a buyer find that his competitor is buying the identical product from the same supplier at a cheaper price or a designer find that his exclusive designs have been copied and marketed by chain stores before they have ever been shown?

As with most diseases − for espionage can be so described − the results need not be critical. The aim is to identify the early symptoms and treat them before the disease takes such a hold that it results in the commercial death of the organisation. Realistic acceptance that if declining sales, leaked promotional details or unsecured tenders, etc, *could* be attributable to industrial espionage then they probably were is an excellent way to proceed. The different kinds of risk, the extent of vulnerability in each case, and the importance of each area for the continuing healthy development of the organisation will all need to be evaluated carefully in the planning stage. Inbuilt defence mechanisms and performance monitors should be sufficiently adaptable and headed with sufficient authority to ensure that timely and effective action is taken to counter them.

2 The Perpetrators

Amateurs

We use the word 'amateur' here to describe people who become involved in espionage, usually against their employer, and who, at some time or another, may be paid in cash or kind for their efforts. We draw a distinction between this type of operator and the type who is trained in the techniques of industrial espionage and earns a living from the proceeds.

'Loyal' employees

People are the most valuable asset of any organisation. However strong or financially secure an organisation may be, its development and survival is almost wholly dependent upon the skills and dedication of its employees. The more skilful and dedicated an employee, the more critical his or her continuing loyalty is to the operation.

Even though prudent personnel selection techniques may have been employed at the recruitment stage and a competent job done on pre-employment 'vetting', no employer is entitled to assume that he has 'bought' an employee's loyalty for life. People change, as does their work and their home environment. Their expectations and fears are affected by all kinds of factors only a few of which an employer has any control over. A hitherto loyal employee can sometimes start to behave in a way which could not reasonably have been anticipated.

It is very rare for employees to be 're-vetted' in a planned and professional way. Most employers do not know if their employees continue to hold the attitudes which they held when they were recruited.

Furthermore, initial screening processes may not take account of the potential for promotion. For example, someone recruited as an accountant could eventually become financial director; however, even if the personnel selection and pre-employment screening took account of the possibility of promotion to such a level, which realistically seems unlikely, the question remains as to what has happened to that person in the ten years or so it has taken him to reach that position – a position of both actual and potential power, making the individual one of the first to know of any major shift in the policy, operation and development of the organisation. The financial director would be one of the first to know if his organisation was going to budget a considerable sum of money for a research project, a new promotion, the acquisition of new plant, technology, premises or other companies. Who better to know the ramifications and probable outcome of any projected takeovers?

It may be that 90 per cent of those whose career follows such a pattern would be absolutely loyal and totally dedicated to the employer who had rewarded him fairly and well. But what of the employee who in the course of reaching the office of financial director, has become a 'risk' because of uncontrollable drinking or gambling? What of the individual with an urgent need for money which he cannot, or chooses not to, raise through normal commercial channels? Even the most loyal employee could be the victim of a blackmail attempt and need to raise money secretly.

Amongst the other 10 per cent there may be some who were passed over for promotion; the salesman who did not get the prestigious company car he expected or was not included in the sales jamboree in the Canary Islands; the employee who did not get the Christmas bonus he had expected – and had already spent; the employee whose daughter, if he could not afford to send her, would be the only one in her class who would not be going on the educational Mediterranean cruise.

It is said that everyone has his price, and this does not necessarily imply corruption. Anyone taking a job 'sells' his skills (and presumably his loyalty) to his employer; he accepts a 'price' in the form of salary, conditions and other benefits for the work he performs.

Even 'loyal' employees faced with an urgent need for money may decide to sell their loyalty. A desperate person does not necessarily think rationally and may well suddenly discover that of all his assets the one which will provide the greatest funds most easily is information which belongs to his employer and is of great value to a rival concern. Every employer must recognise the fact that certain circumstances could render him vulnerable, and he should protect employees against themselves and guard what is his, both by systems and physical security.

Certain employees may approach rival organisations to sell their 'secrets'; but it can also happen that the approach is made to them by the rival organisation or by persons acting on its behalf. If such an approach is not taken up at the time and is never reported, the individual will still remember it and may be tempted to pursue the offer at a later date if his circumstances change.

The danger signals

It was said earlier that an employer should be aware of factors in the work environment that might create disaffection; an obvious example is the effect on a loyal employee of being passed over for promotion. The particular circumstances will dictate how the situation can be helped by restructuring of the department, redefining jobs or changing job titles. In extreme cases it may be prudent to arrange for a 'wronged' employee to be transferred to other duties or temporarily assigned to a less sensitive job until his reaction to the 'wrong' can be judged.

It is an employer's responsibility to ensure that the power struggles which must take place in all businesses do not leave loyal employees bearing a grudge − albeit an unjustified one so far as the employer is concerned. An employer must, for instance, be able to foresee the effect on certain sales staff of refusing them the type of business car owned by their peers in similar organisations. Even the distribution of minor 'perks' such as eligibility for special dining facilities, size of office, size of desk, or having the key to the executive toilet may, in certain cases, cause rancour and predispose an individual to disaffect.

The prudent employer will be seen to act fairly, ensuring that any moves which might appear illogical or unfair are fully justified and explained. He will not overlook the effect which the commissioning of new plant or the institution of new equipment or procedures may have on some employees. Uncertainty and suspicion can cause demoralisation and eventually subversion. Most employees will tend to be opposed to change and very suspicious of any new machine which does the work of several people.

One case of criminal damage to a tanker at sea involved the cutting of critical cables linking experimental and highly sophisticated unmanned space (UMS) equipment from the engine room to the bridge. The system was capable of monitoring and signalling various functions in the engine room and relaying them to the officer of the watch on the bridge. Those investigating the crime had to consider that everyone apart from the captain could have had a motive. The captain, like the managing director of a company, would have had no reason to sabotage the very institution for which he was responsible. Suspicion fell equally upon the engineering officers who may have seen the UMS equipment as a threat to their traditional role and employment and upon the deck officers who may have seen the equipment as another responsibility which they would have to carry with no compensatory pay increase. In fact the culprit proved to be a chief petty officer who had numerous personal problems and was under the influence of alcohol at the time. Although in this case the significance of the equipment itself played no part in motivating the crime, the widespread misgivings and suspicions which had been allowed to develop amongst the crew should have been cause for alarm. There should always be full consultation with the affected personnel before, during and after the institution of any new machinery, equipment or procedures.

Many nations legislate to ensure that an employer provides a healthy and safe work environment for his employees, but there is no such requirement for him to consult his employees on matters concerning the progress and profitability of his organisation. However, it is unwise to rely on the belief that a general does not consult every private in his army before he decides to advance. Consultation with employees in order to gain their commitment and support is vitally important. Failure to consult adequately might result in the demise of the organisation.

Danger signals should, therefore, be obvious to any prudent employer regarding situations over which he has control in the work environment. The success of how they are handled depends on the perception of management, its style of management and the consideration it shows toward its employees, in a world which is increasingly motivated by greed and thirst for power with scant regard for business ethics, decency and honesty.

What of the personal lives of employees? Only a blinkered management would take the view that what an employee did in his private life was of no concern to his employer.

In many occupations there is little truly private life. For example, a solicitor or doctor will be bound by codes of conduct which affect his private life almost as stringently as his professional life. Any successful person in the commercial world acquires a life style and material possessions which are obvious to those around him in his private life, and status and job become inseparable from the individual. People tend to seek the company of others of similar status, and this shows in their choice of clubs, hotels, pursuits and activities. Behavioural norms are thus established, and any significant departure from a norm may be regarded with suspicion. A person apparently living well below what would be expected of one of his status and income is just as suspicious as a person apparently living beyond his means.

Extreme behavioural changes in an individual should be cause for concern. Addiction to alcohol or gambling are obvious pointers to a threatened business life since such activity, which suggests character defects, is almost certainly going to extend to the working environment. There the manifestations are almost certain to include a loss of efficiency and effectiveness, possibly leading to a need for more money.

Domestic disharmony is another factor which can disastrously affect an individual's work performance. Matrimonial problems can sometimes render a person incapable of dealing with the pressures of work.

We do not suggest that an employer should set

himself up as a super sleuth-cum-psychiatrist, or employ paid informers, but it is important that consideration is given to identifying employee problems which could become employer problems, and to prevent this happening. Personnel departments of larger organisations may well have the necessary expertise, and should be encouraged to concern themselves with the welfare and problems both official and personal of employees. There is more to the personnel function, of course, than hiring and firing. What happens between these events is equally important.

An organisation's own medical department may provide valuable and timely indications of personal problems affecting health and efficiency, and the security department may also make useful observations. In line management different levels of supervision exist, but responsibility for an individual's work performance should always include some responsibility for the individual. A caring company will always get to know something of its employees' personal lives and how their performance may be affected. An environment where people are encouraged to discuss their problems, grievances, fears and expectations is a healthy one in which deceit and dishonesty find it difficult to flourish.

With the right management and management style, there need be no opposition to regular background vetting, particularly if it is understood that the checks apply to all personnel and are to the advantage of everyone.

To summarise, openness in management style, encouragement to share success and disappointment, joy and disaster with line managers, assisted, when available, by security, personnel or medical departments — these are the most important factors in creating a climate in which people are least likely to be susceptible to subversion.

The temporary employee

The temporary employee is another source of potential
risk. Many large companies, particularly multination-
als, play the 'head count game', in which success is
measured by the number of employees on the payroll —
the fewer the better. Temporary workers, who cost
more to employ, are taken on so that the organisation
can function properly. This is considered to be desirable because they are not actually on the payroll. It
may be felt, for instance, that five architects are
necessary in a department; to reduce the head count,
four will be made redundant and immediately replaced
by four temporary architects who, paradoxically, will
cost more to employ. The value of this kind of exercise
is extremely doubtful.

From a security point of view, one needs to ask
where the loyalty of any temporary employee lies. The
answer must be that his first loyalty is to his immediate
employer, that is the agency or firm that contracts him
to the client. Where and for whom he works is of
secondary importance which is why such persons,
particularly if employed in a sensitive work area, are a
constant threat to security. Moreover, the employer
will know far less about the background of such
employees since one advantage of employing them is
that, if they are unsatisfactory, he just has to ask the
agency to remove and replace him. It is possible for a
temporary worker to be employed for just a few days in
an organisation to which he has little or no loyalty, with
every opportunity to appropriate and abuse confidential information if the employer is lax.

The area where temporary employees are most
common is among secretarial staff, and there has been
a rapid growth over the last few years of agencies
dealing in secretarial skills.

It is an unfortunate characteristic of most businessmen who are entitled to a secretary that in order not to lose that entitlement and the status which accompanies it, they will try to get a temporary secretary whenever their permanent one is on holiday, regardless of whether the workload justifies it. Thus, at holiday time companies which have followed prudent selection, vetting and training procedures throughout the rest of the year throw their doors wide open to all sorts of 'strangers' who may have the appropriate secretarial skills but are employed mainly because they 'look right'. Many temporary agency staff feel very little loyalty except to themselves and are prime targets for subversion since they risk so little in the unlikely event that they are detected. The fact that they are in new surroundings makes it especially easy for them to ask questions and seek information which naturally helpful and unsuspecting established employees will normally give gladly. 'Unusual' behaviour may well be over-looked on the basis that − 'she's only a temporary and is trying to find her way round.' Clients or customers who ring into the company where the temporary answers the phone are not to know that she is someone to whom they should not be speaking openly − after all, she answers the telephone.

Another danger is that male office staff will often go out of their way to assist an attractive temporary secretary; they may impart all sorts of confidential information in the hope of convincing her of their own importance. The nature and scope of some secretarial duties make it possible for a great deal of damage to be inflicted upon a temporary employer.

It would seem to be advisable for temporary absence of secretarial staff to be covered either by sharing the work amongst other established secretaries or by promoting temporarily or re-assigning a less senior secretary. A temporary should only be employed if one is really required on routine and non-sensitive work.

The enthusiastic 'boffin'

Some experts just have to discuss their latest achievements. This is a perfectly natural tendency, but it can be dangerous. Unfortunately, people who are very talented in their own specialised sphere are sometimes lacking in common sense or circumspection especially when they have achieved a breakthrough in something with which they have been preoccupied for a considerable time. Scientists tend to be difficult people to warn of the need for secrecy.

It is natural for anyone to wish to explain to family or friends what his job is and how well he is doing it, and specialists thrive on 'talking shop'. It is fundamental to discourage any sensitive 'shop talk' in public places, but there is an area of greater danger than this. All professions have their own societies and associations which hold meetings, seminars or training sessions. The greatest vulnerability for any specialist employee is when he is attending such a gathering. There the talk will tend to be about the particular projects and methods of work. What more natural than for two people who perhaps went through university together to tell one another in great detail just what they are doing now? What more natural than an ex-employee meeting an old colleague and catching up with what has been going on since he left?

People attend professional meetings to gain information; but they may unwittingly be imparting information which will be turned to the disadvantage of the originator.

Discussion of sensitive subjects should definitely not take place when the parties have had a lot to drink. Scientists and chemists, particularly when they are involved in sensitive, costly and lengthy research projects, are a specific high risk area. Special effort should be provided to educate and warn them of the need for circumspection in their work.

The employee with a grudge

If communications are good within a company there should not be any employees with a grudge against their employer which he does not know about. Once the employer is aware of a grievance, he can take appropriate action like changing job titles or descriptions or transferring to other duties. But if a deep-rooted feeling of injustice remains, particularly if there is also a problem outside work, this may cause the employee to try to get his own back on his employer.

People working for large and impersonal employers often feel more or less entitled to steal goods from the company — 'They're so big they won't miss it'; 'They've got more than they need'; 'I deserve more than they pay me, so this helps to redress the balance'. To counteract this kind of thinking, most companies which manufacture or sell products which their staff might buy offer them a discount on any purchases they make. However, no such concessions will appease an employee who bears a strong grudge. And that individual might decide that selling or even giving sensitive information to a rival provides him with the greatest revenge.

Professionals

'Plants'

A company wanting to obtain confidential information from a rival may think it unlikely that it will be able to buy the services of a key employee, in which case, other methods are available.

We have already mentioned the ease with which temporary staff can gain access to confidential files and information, and a professional sponsor will find opportunities to 'plant' his man or woman in the target company.

The types of temporary staff that may be engaged include technical support staff, architects, technical draughtsmen, computer staff, laboratory technicians and, of course, secretarial staff.

With proper briefing, experienced operatives can, in a matter of days, obtain information which may have taken their victim years and considerable sums of money to acquire. Successful operatives enjoy a glamorous image and are well rewarded financially. Meanwhile, to add insult to injury, their temporary employer is paying the going rate for their ostensible services − a double punishment for the victim!

'Sleepers'

'Sleepers' are usually associated with international espionage, but where the stakes are high enough, they are also used in the commercial field. They are professional spies, usually with high academic and the appropriate professional qualifications who are 'introduced' into a company which has been singled out for penetration. They apply for a genuinely advertised vacancy, and their qualifications make it a virtual certainty that they will be offered the position.

The sleeper will work in the organisation for a number of years, exhibiting apparent loyalty and no doubt contributing to its fortunes. However, all the time he will be paid and controlled by his ultimate master. After, say, four or five years, when the sleeper has reached a position of considerable influence in the organisation, he commits an act of treachery designed to destroy the organisation. The proceeds of such chicanery would obviously be substantial if they resulted in the company being taken over at a falsely deflated price.

If the subterfuge is a complete success, the sleeper will emerge as a personally successful executive, unlucky enough to be involved in an inexplicable commercial disaster. He can then proceed confidently to seek employment elsewhere, although it is unlikely that he would be able − or would want − to be introduced as a sleeper again.

False head-hunters

Another very successful way of securing sensitive information which is increasingly used is by pretending to head-hunt.

An individual in the rival organisation is 'targeted'. This means that he becomes the subject of detailed research which enables the perpetrator to design a false but totally credible vacancy in a 'large international organisation' absolutely tailor-made to attract the intended victim. In compiling a picture of the victim, the researcher may contact professional bodies which will freely provide much detailed background; and inquiries undertaken by a private investigator will elicit details of private life, hobbies, pastimes, habits, etc.

The position may then be advertised in the appropriate trade or professional journal. If the targeted person applies, well and good − the trap is sprung. If he does not apply for the vacancy, an agent will contact the person at his place of work or home, introducing himself as a consultant, head-hunting for a client. He will stress the extreme secrecy of his assignment and will suggest that it would be to their mutual advantage to continue their conversation in a place where privacy can be assured. Arrangements will then be made to meet at a prestigious hotel.

If the agent has done his homework carefully, he will know the full background of his victim and exactly what is likely to interest him in terms of alternative employment. As is customary, the 'head-hunter' will not divulge the name of the company on whose behalf he is seeking the employee. If, for instance, the victim shows a desire for travel, vague references may be made to the company's international interests, suggesting a need for frequent trips. Pay and conditions of service offered will, of course, be vastly superior to those the individual is already known to enjoy. Throughout the initial interview much stress will be placed upon the mutual need for absolute secrecy in the negotiations because of the delicacy of the whole matter. An air of mystery is deliberately created to favour the 'head-hunter'.

If the bait is taken and a rapport is successfully established, a second interview is arranged. Another person will then be present with the 'head-hunter', purporting to be the client's representative. He will be a specialist in the victim's own field of knowledge, and thus capable of extracting the technical information which is desired.

The victim will, it is hoped, by now be so keen to impress his interviewers that he will overcome any misgivings about divulging sensitive information. He will talk freely and openly, prompted where necessary by the interviewer. Carefully planned and rehearsed sessions of this type may well secure all of the information required. If not, a further interview (reflecting the vast importance of the position offered) may be arranged, perhaps with another person present. The information will have been 'bought' for the price of a hotel room.

If the 'head-hunter' is asked for a name or telephone

number, it may be possible to persuade the victim that this cannot be provided on the grounds of confidentiality, or to use an 'accommodation' contact point.

It does occasionally happen that the company which has perpetrated this kind of deceit ends up by offering the 'applicant' a genuine job. However, the usual outcome is that the person is simply informed that his application has not been successful. What is worse, he may subsequently find himself the object of a blackmail attempt because of his disloyalty in divulging secret information belonging to his employer.

Eavesdropping

Restaurants, bars, public houses, trains and taxis are all places where the indiscreet engage in the most sensitive conversations. Offering a waiter an incentive to 'listen out' for any information which might be disclosed in a restaurant known to be frequented by members of a rival organisation often pays off. It was partly to discourage the press from eavesdropping on conversations between detectives that Scotland Yard established their own public house, 'The Tank', from which the public are excluded.

Another opportunity which is sometimes taken to pick up information is to book a seat on a train close to a party travelling to or from a meeting. Useful eavesdropping can also be done by the driver of a taxi who contrives to pick up, say, members of conference.

It is remarkable how often visitors are left alone in offices. Anybody with a natural curiosity might have a good look at information displayed on walls such as bar charts, graphs, drawings, and so on; while trained observers might take the opportunity to scrutinise a file or record carelessly left out on a desk. Reading 'upside down' is a useful and easy technique to learn which often helps to avoid suspicion.

While all the above practices will produce some information, results are bound to be variable and even unreliable; a far greater threat to confidentiality is posed by the use of bugging devices. Once access has been gained to a particular office or operating area one of many different types of instrument can be installed to transmit conversations to a recorder or to a live listening post. These devices are described fully in Chapter 4.

The ultimate professionals

In the perpetual power struggle between East and West there exists not only military intelligence but, so far as the Soviet Union is concerned, an equally efficient body whose sole aim is the acquisition of Western technology and expertise by legal and illegal means. It is sponsored by the State and its members are KGB officers. At Zelongrad, just northwest of Moscow, is the Soviet state manufacturer of micro chips for use in integrated circuits, many of which have both military as well as civil applications. The Soviet government is considerably dependent upon Western technology in this field and has had significant success in purloining American technology, in particular both equipment and plans from San Francisco's Silicon Valley.

The US authorities, in attempting to curb the flow of sensitive equipment to the Soviet Union, drew up a list of embargoed commodities to prevent their export to the Soviet Union. However, the financial stakes were so high that it was not long before the embargoes were being circumvented. Sensitive material, with a considerable military capability, produced in Silicon Valley, was being shipped to West Germany on documents describing it as washing machines or machinery; it was then sold on to southern Germany or the Austrian border, transported overland to East Germany and then presumably to the Soviet Union. The West German airline Lufthansa took many such consignments from Los Angeles to Munich, Vienna or Switzerland — consignments which were subsequently transported overland to the East.

The US authorities required such equipment to carry a certificate that it was to remain in the first destination country. Certificates were easily obtainable and non-compliance was virtually impossible to detect or punish. Goods destined for the East were frequently misdescribed, and a bewildering variety of names and locations were used in attempts to confuse and conceal the nature of the shipment. As intermediaries were being paid three times the US cost of the equipment, it is little wonder that few difficulties were encountered.

In 1984 it also transpired that the Moscow Narodny Bank, through a series of manoeuvres — many executed through Hong Kong — were systematically buying up numerous small American banks which operated in the San Francisco (Silicon Valley) area, utilising finance obtained at very low interest rates. Having acquired the small banks which had hitherto been financing the US micro chip companies, the Soviet Union was in a position to uncover sensitive details about various manufacturers, and also, for example, to pinpoint engineering employees with financial difficulties whom they might be able to suborn. As Lenin said:

'The capitalists will sell us the rope to hang the West.'

Conclusion

It is depressing to realise how many people can be persuaded to disloyalty, for any number of reasons and by many different means. Some of the temptations and incentives can and should be identified. Others may not be apparent.

Prevention is always better than detection, and a prudent employer should deal with an employee's personal problems or misdeeds with sensitivity and compassion. That is not to imply that an employer should appear weak. For example, where theft from the employer is involved company policy should insist on prosecution and dismissal. The probability of detection and the certainty of prosecution and dismissal are fair to employer and employee alike.

There is no substitute for good management and an awareness of how and why the company's secrets can be put at risk.

3 Acquiring Secret Information

The most useful way of obtaining information from a secret document, plan, sketch, drawing or design is to 'borrow' it. If it can be removed from its normal place without arousing suspicion, taken to the person interested in it for examination, photographed or photocopied, then both the spy and his principal can be sure that the right article has been obtained and the critical data secured. The article can be returned from whence it came and the true owner should not learn of its temporary loss until it is too late to do anything about it.

An otherwise loyal employee might be persuaded to take part in this kind of activity, by convincing himself that all he had to do was to borrow something and return it, while someone else did the dirty work of copying it! This method of acquiring secret information may seem to offer the lowest chance of detection and the best chance of success. It is easy, for example, to take a document, or even a file, out of an office building in a brief case; it is unlikely to be detected even if there happens to be the sort of exit check occasionally carried out by security personnel.

Visitors

Visitors to business premises are often not treated with sufficient caution. All visitors should be required to report to a reception desk at the point of entry to a building, before they can proceed to a lift or staircase inside the building. The bonafides of the visitor should be confirmed by the receptionist by telephoning the person with whom he has an appointment. The visitor should then be escorted to, or collected by, the person concerned.

It is all too easy for an industrial spy, or indeed a walk-in thief, having gained access to a building, to make a note of a name or office title on a door so that if and when he is challenged he can plausibly claim to be looking for that office. Most helpful employees will re-direct the person without suspicion.

Any temporary identity card or badge issued to visitors should be clearly displayed, and all employees should be encouraged to challenge any person they see within the building who is unknown to them without a visitor badge. Temporary identity cards or badges must be recorded and signed for on issue and collected and signed back on departure. Many organisations put their security at risk by failing to ensure that such passes are properly collected or accounted for.

Proper registration and control of visitors is not only of significant security value; it also ensures that in the event of an emergency such as a fire, there is a record of who is in the building and precisely where they are.

Contractors

To gain access to targeted premises professional spies may disguise themselves as the sort of contractor whom most employees would not regard with suspicion. If this did not look to be a feasible way of gaining access he might instead get himself taken on by a contractor who had a legitimate access to the building or even bribe an established contractor to do the job for him. Office cleaners, window cleaners, telephone cleaners, florists, maintenance workers, service engineers are all easily imitated and an impostor can normally go about his work without hindrance.

It is a laborious process, but the prudent organisation will insist that it has a list of all workers likely to be employed on the contract so that their acceptability can be checked and temporary passes issued.

Contract cleaners usually work before or after normal working hours. It is essential that when supervision is minimal all safes, filing cabinets, desk drawers, etc are properly secured. Any area where such security is impossible or impractical, such as an EDP centre, requires the attendance of a member of staff whilst the contractor is on site.

Security risks in the office

The contents of waste paper bins, particularly those in sensitive areas, are of great importance and interest to industrial spies. Effective paper shredders should be placed in areas of high security risk, especially close to photocopiers where discarded and near perfect copies may otherwise frequently be found.

It is pointless to provide good physical security for confidential reports if the secretary who took the original details in her shorthand notebook leaves that lying about on the top of her desk. After transcription the shorthand notes should be torn out and shredded, and if they were typed on a 'once only' typewriter ribbon, it too should be properly destroyed in a commercial shredder or incinerator since it is very easy to read.

Graphs, bar charts, designs or anything else of

proprietary value should not be displayed on walls in offices where they can be seen and evaluated by unauthorised persons. Similarly, training, briefing and conference rooms should be thoroughly checked after a meeting to make sure that no discarded hand-outs or handwritten notes are left lying around. Such items should be destroyed if their owners do not want them. Care should also be taken to secure transparencies and slides, the carousel, and any other visual display material that could be valuable to a rival company. This is particularly necessary after board meetings. There is a story, which may be apocryphal, of a board room in which had been placed a portable letter box with the inscription 'For Confidential Waste'. The only problem was that it was placed there and collected after meetings by an industrial spy who had found an excellent means of intelligence gathering!

Business trips

When executives travel on company business and stay overnight in hotels they present much easier targets for spies.

Something of the 'little boy' tends to emerge in many businessmen when they are away from their normal environment of office and home. The combination of the fact that they are in a town where they are not known and the fact that they are living on expenses can turn normally mild-mannered and dedicated company servants into heavy drinking, free spending individuals intent on having a good time.

What appears to be a casual encounter with an attractive, well-spoken woman in the hotel or bar could well be the deliberate introduction of a professional spy. In such circumstances many men, eager to impress, will cast caution to the wind and with a combination of fact and boastful exaggeration, provide a skilled questioner (or listener!) with enormous amounts of information. Such a meeting, however innocent the traveller may subsequently recollect it to have been, could be the basis for future blackmail by threats of disclosure to office or home. A skilled operator will ensure that something will occur at the encounter whose disclosure could cause embarrassment.

A person travelling to a meeting is almost certain to carry with him in his briefcase all the papers necessary for the meeting (very conveniently selected for the spy). Whereas some travellers may think to secure their personal valuables in the hotel safe or deposit box, most would not consider the contents of their briefcase to be vulnerable to theft or unauthorised disclosure.

Briefcases are frequently left in unattended hotel rooms. Any reasonably competent and plausible spy (or thief) can usually gain access to the hotel room. Many hotels just hand a room key over to anyone who asks for it without further question. It is easy to find out which room the target person is occupying and to observe when he deposits his key (usually in a collecting box) and is obviously going out for the evening. A spy might decide that circumstances make it worthwhile actually taking a room in the same hotel, so that if he is challenged when asking for the wrong key, he has the perfect excuse of having made a mistake.

Helpful housekeeping staff and porters are often the unwitting accomplices of spies. They will open a room door with their pass key if the request to do so seems reasonable − 'I've just handed my key in to reception, to save me going all the way back, could you?' − and a good tip is offered.

Combination locks of the type now standard on the so-called executive briefcase are no deterrent to the spy or thief. Sometimes the code will be guessed (particularly if it is 000 or 123!), but in any case a well-placed screwdriver will force the poor quality lock possibly without leaving any sign that it has been tampered with. Even if the lock is ruined, the owner may simply satisfy himself that nothing is missing and conclude that it must have jammed in normal use.

For a businessman abroad the hazards are multiplied. Not only are the temptations greater but a skilled operator can use local knowledge of laws, customs and procedures to ensnare the stranger. For example, few visitors to Malaysia would know that there is a law called khalwat, enforced by the police, and based on the Muslim beliefs; this law makes it an offence for unmarried men and women to be together unchaperoned and in 'close proximity' − for example, sitting together on a park bench or even driving or parked alongside each other. The penalties are severe; unmarried couples are required to marry; if one party is already married, there are heavy fines and/or imprisonment.

Printers

Companies which have material printed or have printing blocks made by outside specialists, need to beware of the inherent dangers. There is always the possibility that the printer will have contracted to do a similar job for a competitor as the one he has agreed to do for you. This may give rise to a conflict of interests, but the more common security problem arises from the fact that a printer is unlikely to be as concerned about security as the person placing the job. Discarded or rejected proofs of new promotional material are likely to end up in the dustbin − a great source for the industrial spy!

Publicity

Publicity material, press statements and particularly photographs all need to be scrutinised from a security standpoint by the chief executive or at least a board member with knowledge of or responsibility for security before being released to the press or public. PROs may not be able to judge exactly what information should be published. There is a delicate balance to be struck between what a company should proudly proclaim to the world and what should remain confidential. The openly published material of many a large organisation provides its rivals with much useful weaponry.

Investigative journalists can be particularly aggressive as they compete with each other for sensational stories. Any requests for interviews should be referred to one person in the company, and everybody else should be discouraged from saying anything that could subsequently embarrass the company.

4   *Espionage Techniques*

It may be an over-simplification to state that most people in a business environment are motivated by greed and lust. Certainly these appetites, manifested in one form or another, are the cause of a great deal of harm. They are powerful factors in crimes which frequently lead to personal and/or financial ruin for both instigator and victim.

A now high ranking police officer once told me that after his first two years in the force he told a superior: 'I've done nothing but fornicate and get drunk since I've been in this job'. His superior replied: 'Well, you're getting paid for it!' This somewhat paraphrased anecdote seems to suggest that what makes the world go round is money, sex and drink.

The American behavioural psychologist Douglas McGregor in his book *The Human Side of Enterprise* concerned himself with what motivates people in a work environment. He illustrated two differing views of man in relation to his work. The Theory X man, lacking in ambition, who inherently dislikes work, avoiding it if he can, and who has to be coerced, controlled, directed or threatened with punishment in order to perform reasonably well; and the Theory Y man who regards physical and mental effort in work as natural as play and rest, who is keen to learn and eager to take responsibility and maximise his potential both individually and for his employer.

People engaged in espionage seek to change their victim's motivation in order to suborn an otherwise loyal employee. Although new and more sophisticated technical aids to espionage are becoming available all the time, it is people themselves who remain the focus of attention. People are very often of greater value to the commercial spy than the actual things they are responsible for creating and in which the spy is ultimately interested. To 'buy' the individual is to 'buy' his secrets, present and future; a much better proposition than to 'steal' one piece of proprietary information.

Secretaries

The man himself may be too difficult a subject for subversion: no hint of instability, dissatisfaction or vulnerability. However, his personal assistant or secretary may be a much easier prospect.

Many senior executives' secretaries are mature women who have sacrificed a normal married relationship for their career. They have found themselves unable to handle the conflicting loyalties and responsibilities of home and work. Sometimes desperately lonely when not at work, they make excellent targets for the personable male flatterer who can contrive to be in the right place at the right time and who sets out to win their friendship, confidence and eventual loyalty.

Senior secretaries have a lot of power. Many derive their own sense of importance from the importance of their boss's job. Competition between them can be as intense as that between their bosses. When the promotion process goes against them, they can make promising targets for espionage.

Many ambitious junior employees will attempt to ingratiate themselves with their boss's secretary in the hope of picking up useful confidences. Such secretaries are that much more vulnerable to approaches made by a professional operator able to spend large sums of money on lavish entertainment, gifts and other blandishments.

Market research

Market research is a quite legitimate activity, engaged in by manufacturers and others to assess the present or future success of a product or service. But it can also be used in a more sinister way, to get people to talk on virtually any subject at great depth and without arousing undue suspicion. The appeal to answer questions when you are told that you have been selected out of thousands or that the organisation promoting the survey (probably never named!) will be rewarding some participants with expensive prizes may be irresistible.

The 'market research canvasser' is a cover frequently used by investigators employed to do pre-employment vetting since it affords the opportunity to interview an individual or a member of the family without provoking answers and reactions which a formal pre-employment interview might.

Bribery and threats

Once an employee has been persuaded to indulge in some dubious activity or has accepted a gift or service which, by any definition, is lavish and makes his loyalty to his employer questionable, the way is open for the perpetrator to tighten his hold on the traitor by making the most of the weakness or indiscretion.

Many people who embark on fraud only continue their involvement because of threats of disclosure by another participant. Others simply find that fraud has become a way of life, and the income derived from it has become a necessity. Almost all frauds commence in a modest way but grow rapidly as the 'system' appears to stand the test of time and the perpetrators' confidence grows.

There was a case in a major oil company where a computer operator, just to see if it would work, processed falsely inflated discounts on the price of petrol delivered to a garage. Not only did it work but the system seemed almost undetectable. It was not long before a conspiracy developed between the computer operator in head office and a field salesman who selected those garages that were to receive the inflated discounts. The garages paid part of their savings to the salesman who in turn paid the computer operator for the part he played. Some £27,000 was generated for the conspirators over a period of about three years, the garages and the salesman gaining the lion's share. The computer operator, without whose continued co-operation the fraud would not have been possible, never received more than £50 for a dishonest manipulation of the computer; it was normally only £15 or £20 on a delivery making several hundred pounds for the others. The fraud was eventually detected and prison sentences and substantial fines were meted out to the participants.

The tragedy for the computer operator was that he was a young and inexperienced man, who only perpetrated the first fraud 'to test the system and see if it could be done'. Once he had accepted money for his success, although he did not want to continue, he was threatened with disclosure by the older and more dominant salesman and so the fraud grew.

Since industrial espionage, like other frauds, involves

the giving and taking of bribes, it is maintained from the time the victim is first compromised, continuing inducements or threats of disclosure or a combination of both.

It is not suggested that any member of staff who commits an occasional indiscretion is liable to fall victim to practitioners of espionage, but evidence of frailty or weakness certainly makes him a more likely target. Throughout the world senior politicians, civil servants and service chiefs have been removed from office as a result of scandals involving sexual indiscretion. It is not usually a matter of their sexual affairs affecting their official duties but that their behaviour makes them likely targets for blackmail and subornation. The government of the United Kingdom was brought down in 1963 because of the association of the Secretary of State for War, John Profumo and the prostitute Christine Keeler who was also involved with the Soviet Naval Attaché, Captain Eugene Ivanov. There was no proof that British military secrets had been passed to Ivanov either by Profumo or by Keeler, but the situation was potentially extremely dangerous.

Optical aids

Binoculars and telescopes used to be the basic equipment, but in conditions of bad light or darkness, definition would be poor or non-existent. Now, using invisible infra-red beams, it is possible to illuminate subjects which are in darkness so that they appear almost to be in broad daylight.

Night becomes day with a model small enough to be hand-held, incorporating its own rechargeable power source which will run for one and a half hours and cover a range of up to 500 metres; the whole equipment packs neatly into a standard briefcase. More powerful tripod mounted infra-red searchlights can be employed where appropriate to give greater light in circumstances where noctovisors (night vision equipment) are used.

Infra-red projectors can be linked to cameras and videos to provide still or moving pictures of what can be lit by the invisible rays.

Normal flashlight attachments for single lens reflex cameras only have a range of some 10 metres at night. However, with a long-range infra-red flash device it is possible to extend the range to 100 metres without detection since the 'flash' cannot be seen by the human eye because of an IR filter which only lets through the invisible infra-red part of the light.

Secret − that is silent and invisible − flashlight photography is now achieved quite simply in total darkness.

Binoculars can be obtained which contain both night vision equipment and the capability of recording distances and dimensions of the objects viewed by means of an instantaneous digital display. Their use at secret installations is invaluable if an undetected approach can be made to the perimeter under cover of darkness.

Pin hole cameras (endoscopes) now exist with optical shafts as fine as a needle. These can be used through minute holes drilled in walls or furniture and with fibre optics, they can even 'see round bends'. They can be used to film or to record on video; they are virtually undetectable and can be adapted to allow observation in total darkness.

Cameras can be so small now that they fit into a cigarette lighter which actually works. Such a camera might have an electronically controlled shutter speed ranging from 1/500 to 8 seconds and a depth of focus ranging from 1 metre to infinity; it will allow 12, 24 or 36 exposures, depending on the cassette loaded.

Cameras are also capable of being concealed in and operated from a briefcase, a handbag, box file, etc; they can be remotely controlled if required. Their size, their automatic and quiet film winding and their electric shutter release make them an indispensable tool for the commercial spy.

There is even a camera small enough to fit into a wrist watch! The watch is only 10mm thick and looks like a conventional LCD display type, complete with start-stop segment and alarm signal. The camera is loaded with a six-exposure film cassette for indoor and outdoor photography.

One-way observation mirrors are sometimes used by an industrial spy. They may be built in to a building or room either prior to occupation or during a period of vacation. One side looks like a normal mirror whereas the other side is transparent allowing observation and photography through it.

If a place of concealment is large enough to secrete a TV camera and transmitter, the camera can be set for continuous recording and the recorded picture can be transferred into a transmitter's IC store. The transmitter converts the picture to a 3kHz signal which is the voice frequency which can then be located anywhere and is connected to the transmitter's telephone line. The receiver picks up the signal and reproduces the picture on the monitor every eight seconds. If required a picture can be frozen on the monitor. The big advantage of this system is that it can operate over an unlimited range and the picture can also be transmitted by an RF radio transmitter.

Audio aids

Telephone bugs and intercepts require some expertise

and a certain amount of time to plant. Access to and knowledge of telephone exchanges, main frames, junction boxes or even the scaling of telegraph poles may be needed.

Changing the screw-in mouthpiece of a telephone to one containing a transmitter can be a risky business. But devices that require connections inside the telephone itself are even more difficult to set up. This type of device will act as a microphone at all times whether the telephone is being used or not. By employing a coded signal generator it is possible to dial the number of the bugged telephone from anywhere in the world without it ringing and monitor subsequent conversations in the room directly through the telephone wires. The ordinary working of the telephone is in no way disturbed.

Micro transmitters, no larger than a grain of rice, are made to look like capacitors of the type usually found in telephones, which makes their detection virtually impossible. They transmit only when the telephone is in use and draw their power from the telephone current.

Nevertheless, transmitters not dependent upon the telephone are preferred by commercial spies. Location, facilities and environmental considerations will determine the choice of transmitter, which may be powered from the mains, giving it a virtually indefinite life, or carry its own batteries. A limpet transmitter can penetrate walls up to 50 centimetres thick and transmit good quality sound up to a distance of 500 metres without cable.

If background noises such as air conditioning or passing traffic make comprehension of a recorded tape difficult, there is a device that can filter out the interference frequencies and bring up speech frequencies.

Micro transmitters can be adapted to fit in everyday articles such as electric wall sockets, TV aerial co-axial cables, pens, lights and watches, and some are so small they can be inconspicuously placed in an article of clothing. There is even a domestic light bulb (which, although it cannot be used as a light source, would arouse no suspicion) capable of recording all conversations in a room and transmitting them some 250 metres. It has the advantage of an indefinite life since it works from the mains socket into which it is plugged.

Transmitters have been found actually plastered into the walls, and they can also be concealed in plastic nails used behind picture hooks, in an upholstered chair or in the spine of a book. Although the operating time of such devices is only approximately 36 hours per battery, they are easily deposited by the temporary visitor and will transmit over a range of 200 metres. Their price is such that rather than attempt to retrieve them either to renew their batteries or after they have done their job, they are abandoned.

Another technique of monitoring conversation in a room uses laser beams. It comprises a laser transmitter and a corresponding laser receiver. A window is selected which can be accessed from a safe point outside. The laser transmitter, whose beam lies in the invisible infra-red waveband, is directed at the window pane and picked up by the laser receiver; the reflected beam is converted into an electric signal which, after filtering and amplification, is fed into earphones and a cassette recorder. Sound waves of speech cause the pane to vibrate slightly. This movement acts like the diaphragm of a microphone and the reflected laser beam trained on it is converted to audible sound. In reasonable environmental conditions good quality speech can be monitored up to a distance of 500 metres from the target window and a set of batteries, if mains supply is not available, will last up to 50 hours. The entire equipment, including earphones, tripods and cassette recorder, can be fitted into a briefcase.

Detection of espionage devices

It should be said that most of the techniques described above are unlawful in most Western countries. Some countries proscribe the manufacture or import of such equipment, others the possession or clandestine use of it; some attempt to license it for approved users. Legislation is made very difficult by the fact that transmitters have a variety of innocuous uses as well, such as in hearing aids for the deaf, baby alarms that allow the remote monitoring of a nursery and in business recording devices for telephones.

Enforcement of any law in this field is a constant problem. Many transmitters can only be detected when they are actually working. This means that the authorities must be able to determine the frequency on which the transmitter is operating, trace its source, and discover where and by whom it is being monitored: a daunting task indeed. Many people find, therefore, that the rewards of industrial espionage are high enough to outweigh the risk of exposure or detection.

In the UK, provision does exist for State interception of communications such as telephone calls. The only law enforcement organisations which can be granted such facilities are the police, HM Customs and Excise and the Security Services. Each application has to be made in writing to the Home Secretary and has to satisfy strict criteria: that the situation is a very serious one, eg murder, large-scale organised crime, serious threat to the economy, anything prejudicial to national security; and that conventional investigative methods either have been tried and failed or would be likely to fail if attempted; and that the facility, if granted, is for a specified length of time and has a high likelihood of success. Applications by the Police are sometimes refused by the Home Secretary, those by HM Customs and Excise rarely and those by the Security Services almost never. None is ever approved unless the request is substantiated by hard evidence and not speculation. The interception, if granted, is made by specialist British Telecom engineers, always at the exchange of the subscriber and never at his actual telephone.

Checklist of risks

Finally, to summarise the risks involved in the normal course of business, let us suppose that, in a typical office containing typical equipment, a senior member of management has just dictated to his secretary some extremely sensitive information about the company. In what ways is this information vulnerable to acts of industrial espionage designed to steal it?

1 The man.
2 The secretary.
3 A bug in the telephone on the desk activated by ambient voice.
4 A bug in the furniture, wall, fittings or contents.
5 The shorthand notebook used.
6 The 'once only' typewriter ribbon used.
7 The carbon paper used.
8 A spoiled photocopy in the waste paper basket.
9 A boom mike directed at the window.
10 Photography by telephoto lens from an office block across the road.
11 A copy in an unlocked filing cabinet.
12 The photographing, copying or theft of a copy by a 'window cleaner', 'maintenance man' or any other impostor.

5　The Law

Many countries have attempted to introduce legislation to deal with problems within the comparatively new field of industrial espionage.

The difficulties in formulating such laws are manifold. The act of obtaining a business secret often amounts to theft, but while the criminal act of theft requires a certain mental element in that the thief must intend permanently to deprive the owner of what he has taken, an industrial secrets thief will not necessarily deprive the owner permanently of his property, he will merely be forcing the owner to share what he knows with another or others.

Another difficulty lies in the nature of the property which, in the case of 'secrets', is generally intangible. It is often impossible to place a monetary value on the loss suffered by the owner. This can only be done by projection and estimation which a criminal court finds hard to evaluate.

Some countries, notably Switzerland, have managed to enact legislation in both civil and criminal spheres to ensure that most known methods of industrial espionage can be dealt with effectively by their courts. Other countries, including the United Kingdom, have no specific substantive offence to deal with industrial espionage which is not, of itself, a crime. The Official Secrets Act may offer redress in a specific type of espionage, generally involving injury to the State. These statutes will not always protect a private business and the Acts themselves are a welter of highly confusing and sometimes contradictory sections and subsections – it is the opinion of many in the legal profession that a coherent consolidating Act is long overdue, and that the present approach is haphazard and highly unsatisfactory.

When someone (an intruder) enters another person's land or building, a nominal or 'bare' trespass is thereby committed. There may be further breaking and entering with the intention of theft. Further acts, such as the breaking open of a locked door, drawer or cabinets, amount to substantive offences under the Criminal Damage Act, 1971 (as amended). The theft by an industrial spy of a piece of paper with negligible intrinsic value, could be carried out without committing any of the above offences. The potential value of what appeared on that piece of paper may not be taken into account by the Criminal Court unless, however, the theft also contravened the Official Secrets Acts.

If a sensitive document were photocopied on the 'target' premises, it would be possible to charge the perpetrator with theft of the photocopying paper (presumably also the property of the victim) and the cost of the electricity used in producing it. Similarly, anybody found using 'bugs' and recording devices which rely on mains power from the offices in which they are secreted could be charged with theft of the electricity used. However, most bugging and recording devices used today carry their own power supply. The criminal law which makes it an offence to use any unlicensed transmitter is therefore the only way of dealing with this kind of espionage.

Legislation dealing with postal and telegraphic communications usually makes unauthorised tampering with the circuits and wires which protect telephones, teleprinters and computer links an offence.

Existing criminal law in the UK can also effectively deal with those who corrupt and allow themselves to be corrupted in connection with their employment. For example, a law dating back to 1906 makes it a criminal offence 'if any agent corruptly accepts or obtains or agrees to accept or attempts to obtain from any person for himself or another any gift or consideration as an inducement for doing or forbearing to do any act in relation to his principal's affairs or business'. It is a like offence for the person offering the bribe.

Beyond the stage of inducement there are equally adequate laws which deal with threats, blackmail and extortion.

Defining the crime

In England and Wales, section 4(1) of the Theft Act 1968 as amended by the Theft Act 1978 refers to 'things in action' as a subject of theft. The Act refers to proprietary rights which can be enforced only by bringing an action and not by taking possession; for example, shares, patents, copyrights, trade marks and debts.

Infringing a patent, copyright or trade mark is not theft. Infringement of copyright is a statutory offence, although the maximum penalty in the Criminal Court for the infringement itself has recently been as low as £50.

A person selling illicit copies of a pop music cassette or video recording does, however, risk far greater penalties as he may be deemed a constructive trustee of the receipts of sale of the pirated copies and could then be charged with theft of the receipts. If the person operated with a companion it could be conspiracy to defraud, and such offences can carry a penalty of life imprisonment.

Infringing a patent or trade mark may not be a crime although a charge of theft could be brought with regard

to the illicit proceeds, and there may be civil remedies
open to the original owner.

Theft of the rights themselves occurs only when the
whole patent, copyright or trade mark is appropriated,
as when a trustee of a patent wrongfully sells it for his
own benefit and is in breach of his fiduciary duty *qua*
trustee.

Industrial or trade secrets would almost certainly not
be regarded as 'property' for the purpose of theft. An
employee who, in breach of contract, communicates his
employer's secret know-how to a third party does not
deprive the employer of the information and he could
not be described as appropriating the secret since a fact
cannot be stolen. Whereas taking a document and
keeping it permanently could be theft, improperly
copying a document and then returning it would not.
Similarly, if two people are involved in abstracting a
document it could be a conspiracy to defraud, but if
they merely gained access without breaking and entering and committed no criminal damage and photographed the document without removing it from the
premises, it is highly doubtful that they would be guilty
of any offence. There would be a nominal trespass but
the damage attendant thereon would be non-existent or
negligible, and litigation would thus not be worthwhile.

In the case of the private detectives, *Withers,* it was
held by the House of Lords that the act of deception
practised by two people was not a conspiracy to
defraud. Although an employee generally has a duty to
keep information related to his job a secret, he has no
other obligation so to do. The object of the inquiry
agents in *Withers* was not to damage the banks by their
deception but to protect their own clients against loss
from uncreditworthy debtors.

If two persons learn a valuable secret process by

deceiving an employee, it is unlikely that this will constitute a conspiracy to defraud, because there is no property in a trade secret. It may be possible to secure a conviction on the basis that it is a conspiracy to cause loss to the employer, if that loss can be shown to be a necessary consequence. If, however, the employee is an officer of the State, there might be said to have been a conspiracy to cause that employee to act contrary to his duty, which is an offence.

Oxford v Moss

In 1976 a civil engineering undergraduate, Paul Moss, at Liverpool University dishonestly obtained the proof of paper for an examination to be held at the university later in the year. He was charged with theft of confidential information from the senate of the university. The magistrate dismissed the charge on the grounds that there had been no appropriation of 'property' within the meaning of the Theft Act.

The prosecutor appealed to the appropriate division of the High Court. Although there was no dispute that the piece of paper was the property of the university and that at no time did Moss intend to steal what is described as 'any tangible element' belonging to the paper, that is to say that he never intended to steal the paper itself, he was borrowing a piece of paper hoping to be able to return it and not be detected in order to gain an unfair advantage. There is no copyright in the proof examination paper. Moreover, although it was conceded that Moss had gravely interfered with the owner's right over the paper, he had not permanently deprived the owner of any intangible property. The appeal was dismissed.

Scott v Commissioner of Police for the Metropolis

It was held that conspiracy to defraud embraces conspiracy to prevent a person making profit that he would otherwise have made although that case involved the unlawful act of infringing a copyright.

The case progressed from the Central Criminal Court to the Court of Appeal Criminal Division and eventually to the House of Lords. The appellant, Scott, was charged with conspiracy to defraud, in particular that he had conspired together and with other persons as might be caused loss by the unlawful copying and distribution of films, the copyright in which and the distribution rights of which belonged to companies and persons other than the said persons so conspiring and by divers, subtle, crafty and fraudulent means and devices. Scott admitted he had agreed with cinema employees to remove temporarily cinema films without the knowledge and consent of the owners of the copyright and/or distribution rights in such films, in order to make copies and to distribute them on a commercial basis.

He appealed on the grounds a) that the conspiracy charged did not involve deceit of the owner of the copyright and/or distribution rights of the films and there could be no conspiracy to defraud without deceit; and b) that the common law offence of conspiracy to defraud had been implicitly abolished by section 32(1)(2) of the Theft Act 1968.

The appeal was dismissed for the following reasons:

1. In his leading judgment Viscount Dilhorne referred to Stephen's *History of the Criminal Law of England* as recognising that 'a fraud may be perpetrated without deceit by secrecy and that an intent to defraud need not necessarily involve an intent to deceive. A person could be convicted of

conspiracy to defraud if it was shown he had agreed with one or more persons to deprive another by dishonest means of something that either was his or to which he was or would or might, but for the fraud, be entitled. Thus, since Scott had agreed with others to inflict, by dishonest means, economic loss on the owner of the copyright and distribution rights of the films it followed that he was guilty of conspiracy to defraud.

2. Section 32(1)(a) of the Theft Act 1968 abolished the common law offence of cheating which was a distinct offence with a narrower scope than that of conspiracy to defraud. This section could not be construed as having abolished the offence of conspiracy to defraud.

The above cases serve to demonstrate the problems which the judiciary encounter − problems which are, to some extent, exacerbated if not caused by the above-mentioned deficiencies in statutory regulation of industrial espionage.

Trespass, or possibly nuisance, may prove appropriate areas of civil law in which to seek redress against a so-called industrial spy. In connection with the subject of civil remedies, it may be of interest here to consider a recent development of some relevance: Anton Piller Orders.

Anton Piller

The facts of this case are now legend. In 1976 the plaintiffs, Anton Piller, were manufacturers of computer parts in Germany. The defendants were their agents. Anton Piller invented a frequency converter.

Three employees of the defendant company came to Anton Piller in Germany and stated 'Our company will send your details to your rivals'. Not unnaturally, Anton Piller therefore wanted an injunction to restrain this. The question arose; could the plaintiffs (Anton Piller) enter and search the defendants' premises for information?

It was held that the Court could grant an injunction and the plaintiffs were indeed allowed to enter, search and seize any relevant documents. This injunction was granted *ex parte*.

It emerged that three conditions need to be satisfied before such an order can be made.

1. There must be an extremely strong *prima facie* case against the defendants.
2. The plaintiff must show the damage will be serious.
3. There must be clear evidence that
   (a) the defendants have incriminating documents in their possession and
   (b) they will destroy these documents if there is an application on notice.

The next important case on this was that of *Universal City Studios v Mukhtar*. This case involved T-shirts bearing the motif 'Jaws' from the famous film of the same name. Mr Mukhtar owned some of these and thereby was breaching the monopoly which Universal City Studios had over the shirts. It was held in this case that *property* could now be seized.

The newest and most exciting development along the Anton Piller line has been brought about by the practice of 'video piracy'. It is now possible to get an Anton Piller order against shops selling pirated videos whereby the videos may be seized. The order can now require a defendant to answer questions revealing from whom the pirated videos were obtained and to whom they are going to be distributed. In a test case, *Rank Film and Video Information Centre, 1981,* the owner of the video shop refused to answer questions or surrender goods, saying he would not answer because it would show he had committed a crime, and citing the general privilege against self-incrimination. His view was upheld by the House of Lords. An apparent stalemate was averted by the passage of section 72 of the Supreme Court Act, 1981 which reversed the decision in the aforementioned case by stating that the privilege against self-incrimination *cannot* be employed in an Anton Piller case.

The current position as to Anton Piller's and the law now seems to be as follows:

1. The Court now insists that an Anton Piller Order and any affidavit should be served by a solicitor in person.
2. The solicitor must explain to the defendant his right to legal advice.
3. The solicitor is to retain in his safe custody any property seized.
4. The solicitor is to give an undertaking as to damages.

Two more recent cases on this are *Emanuel and Emanuel, 1982* and *ITC Film and Video Exchange, 1982.* The first case relating to family law stated that a solicitor may enter and search and seize documents to show the true financial position of a client who is refusing to comply with a request for proper discovery. It seems, however, that it must be fairly certain that the client is likely to flout any court order. The second case involved a court hearing which had been adjourned for the vacation until the new term. In the interim the defendant seized his own file; however, the solicitors were able to get an Anton Piller Order for recovery of the file. The question then arose: could the defendant use the information which he had obtained by improper means? The general position here is that evidence may be used however improperly obtained, but it was held here that obtaining evidence by way of contempt of court was a general exception to this rule.

A typical Anton Piller Order is reproduced in the Appendix. Its relevance to industrial espionage is that an industrial spy may now be obliged to give over any documents or information obtained by his activities and to divulge the sources of that information and the names of any parties to whom the information has been or was to be imparted.

The law in the USA

In the USA the law makes specific provision for the protection of 'privacy'. Thus American law may be contrasted with the somewhat hotchpotch protection offered by the laws of England and Wales, as earlier described.

Bear in mind that the USA, unlike England and Wales, is a collection of States each with its own laws and administration. This may often lead to 'conflict' among various legal jurisdictions when an act (particularly a civil act) has been committed in more than one State or where such acts involve parties domiciled in different States. Some general principles may, however, be identified.

In the United States, courts in most jurisdictions have, sometimes with the aid of legislation, developed a 'tort of invasion of privacy'. Such a notion has its historical roots in an article by Warren and Brandeis (1890, 4 *Harvard Law Review,* 193) prompted by the press coverage of the wedding of the daughter of one of its authors. The article argued for the existence of a right of privacy in tort based, somewhat ironically, on English precedents such as *Prince Albert* v *Strange*. The tort that has developed in the US is defined in the Restatement 2d Torts 1977 para 652A as follows:

1. One who invades the right of privacy of another is subject to liability for the harm resulting to the interests of the other.

2. The right of privacy is invaded by
   (a) unreasonable intrusion upon the seclusion of another ... or
   (b) appropriation of the other's name or likeness ... or
   (c) unreasonable publicity given to the other's private life ... or
   (d) publicity that unreasonably places the other in a false light before the public.

This restatement represents the majority opinion in American jurisdictions.

To the tort one may add the constitutional right to privacy which originated in *Grisewold* v *Connecticut* (1965) 381 US 479 US Supreme Court. In this case the appellants were convicted under a Connecticut statute for giving advice to married persons on contraception. The constitutionality of the statute was challenged under the US Bill of Rights. The Supreme Court struck down as 'unconstitutional' a state statute on the ground that it conflicted with a constitutional right to privacy which is nowhere mentioned in the Bill of Rights and which the Court found hidden in the 'penumbra'. In other words, the Court inferred a *general* right of privacy from the guarantee in the Bill of Rights of *particular* aspects of it. As Douglas J (for the Court) stated:

'... the First Amendment has a penumbra where privacy is protected from Governmental intrusion ...'

The present case then concerns a relationship lying within the zone of privacy created by several fundamental constitutional guarantees. And it concerns a law which, in forbidding the *use* of contraceptives rather than regulating their manufacture or sale, seeks to achieve its goals by means having a maximum destructive impact upon that relationship. Such a law cannot stand in the light of the familiar principle so often applied by this Court, that a 'governmental purpose to control or prevent activities constitutionally subject to State regulation may not be achieved by means which sweep unnecessarily broadly and thereby invade the area of protected freedoms' (*NAACP* v *Alabama* 377 US 288.307 (1964). Would we allow the police to search the sacred precincts of marital bedrooms for telltale signs of the use of contraceptives? The very idea is repulsive to the notions of privacy surrounding the marriage relationship.

'We deal with a right of privacy older than the Bill of Rights – older than our political parties, older than our school system. Marriage is a coming together for better or for worse hopefully enduring and intimate to the degree of being sacred. It is an association that promotes a way of life, not causes; a harmony in living, not political faiths; a bilateral loyalty, not commercial or social projects. Yet it is an association for as noble a purpose as any involved in our prior decisions.'

The attitude which underlies this emotive outpouring typifies a judicial approach which helped to create the basis of the so-called 'US Constitutional right to privacy'. The Supreme Court and lower federal and state courts have since developed this for use in varying contexts – for example: to strike down abortion statutes (*Roe* v *Wade* 410 US 113 (1973) US S Ct); to protect the private possession of obscene films (*Stanley* v *Georgia* 394 US 557 (1969) US S Ct) and unnatural

sex acts within marriage in private (*Cotner* v *Henry* 394
F 2d 873 (7th Cir 1968)); and to permit long hair in
school (*Breen* v *Kohl* 419 F 2d 1034 (7th Cir 1969)); and
marijuana (*Ravin* v *State* 537 P 2d 494 (1975)).

Unlike the USA, the UK has no written constitution
and the desirability of having such a constitution is
often the subject of jurisprudential argument. The UK
is of course subject to Article 8 of the European
Convention of Human Rights (1950 Cmnd 8969):

'1. Everyone has the right to respect for his private
and family life, his home and his correspondence.

2. There shall be no interference by a public
authority with the exercise of this right except
such as is in accordance with the law and is
necessary in a democratic society in the interests
of national security, public safety or the economic well-being of the country, for the prevention
of disorder or crime, for the protection of health
or morals or for the protection of the rights and
freedom of others.'

The proviso in the second part of this Article is a virtual
derogation from the principle enshrined within the first
part and is so nebulous that an invasion of privacy
(particularly by the 'State') could easily be made to
seem justifiable. Furthermore, as with many 'European' remedies, any protection offered by Article 8
would in practice be weakened by the delay and cost of
obtaining redress.

Given that protecting business secrets may be inex-
tricably linked with the general right to privacy, the
protection available in the USA is, at the very least,
more clearly defined than in the UK.

This chapter in no way pretends to cover all aspects
of the law. What it seeks to do is to indicate that in
many cases there is little or no legal redress against

industrial spies. For this reason, amongst others, it is better to prevent breaches of security than to look to the law for rectification after the events.

Part II
Managing The Risk

6 Taking Security Seriously

The benefits of preventive medicine have long been recognised:with regular health checks we can expect to live longer, healthier lives. And we can draw an analogy between the human body and the business organisation. Certain functions within a company are as critical to its survival as the heart and lungs are to the human body, and their health needs to be checked and monitored constantly. A company may be well advised to identify the functions within its organisation and grade them according to their vulnerability and importance.

It may be that funding is seen to be the 'heart' of the organisation, but the heart will not function without the proper supply of blood (cash flow) which is generated from sales of goods or provision of services; these stem from production which requires a mixture of raw materials and work skills. What is made may also be a critical factor, and research and development may play a very important part in keeping the company innovative, up-to-date and competitive, thereby ensuring a constant demand in the market place.

Marketing and sales may, at first, seem to be the most important functions in a company, because without them funds would not be generated to finance the rest of the operation. However, certain supportive functions may be even more critical since they have a direct impact on the volume of sales. For example, a designer in a knitwear company may be seen to have a more critical role than the entire sales force since if the designs are unappealing the best sales team in the world will be unable to sell them and the company will fail. The acquisition of good quality materials, manufacture and cost are also important ingredients, but all are ancillary to the basic requirement of good designs.

If, as in the example above, the design function is regarded as the most critical area in the organisation, then the organisation should direct its greatest effort, support and security protection to that area. The stealing of exclusive designs for adaptation and reproduction in vast numbers by chain stores is an area where commercial spies are highly active.

One way to establish which functions are most vulnerable and critical to the company's success is to conduct a 'SWOT' analysis of the business. That is, each division or department is analysed under the headings Strengths, Weaknesses, Opportunities and Threats. By research and discussion it should be possible to rate the various entries on say a scale of 1 – 10. This will reveal their individual significance; a very high or very low rating will indicate an area in need of support or protection.

Many companies flounder because they tend to forget the business they are in; they go for diversification instead of directing their greatest effort towards what they are best at. The same is true of security measures and counter-measures. Only careful and objective analysis of the critical functions of an organisation will reveal which ones warrant the greatest effort and expense to protect them.

The security committee

Any company which takes its security seriously must be aware of the threat of industrial espionage. A company must know what parts of its organisation are vulnerable, to what degree, and what steps, both protective and reactive, can be taken to maintain security.

The chief executive himself — reflecting the importance of the matter — should head a committee whose specific aim is to analyse the critical functions of the organisation and the points of vulnerability. The rest of the committee do not all have to be board members, in fact there is an advantage if they are not, but they should be senior staff drawn from various departments of the business. To invite senior line managers on to a security committee encourages participation and engenders interest in the subject which for many will be a new one. It might be prudent for a small working party to set out guidelines and procedures for the security committee, before it is set up. The committee should meet quite separately from the board, whose own meetings will be one subject for security consideration. Whereas its meetings should be regular, like all committees it will lose impact if it meets solely 'because it is the first Monday in the month'. Sufficient interest and impetus should soon be created once feedback is established and the whole business of security (including threats of industrial espionage) becomes a live issue.

It is worthwhile occasionally to obtain a guest speaker who specialises in some aspect of security to address the committee. Security consultants, police crime prevention officers, and even fire prevention officers, can be asked not only to conduct a survey but also to deliver a suitable lecture.

An essential function of a security committee is to produce a manual covering the whole range of security situations and details of actions to be taken in the event of a security problem arising.

It is very important to establish a procedure by which personnel should report security matters. Any procedure will obviously lay down who receives the action copy of the report and who receives a copy 'for information'. A typical distribution might be:

Action copy —   Security manager
                 (or the person he reports to)

Information copy — Company secretary
                   Legal advisers
                   Risk management/insurance
                   Financial director/internal audit

Having a reporting system, particularly one which is laid down in an operational manual or company precedent book, does ensure that no person is expected to exercise judgement on his own. If the problem is likely to cause embarrassment to an individual executive this is a vital consideration.

A system which provides for impartial investigation of all incidents acts as a deterrent to managers who might be tempted to cover up mistakes or shortcomings in their department on the grounds that they reflect adversely on their ability to manage.

To ensure that the reporting of incidents does not become too cumbersome, a minimum value of loss can be set for reporting to a certain level in the hierarchy. Care needs to be taken to ensure that a non-reporting requirement does not mask a continuing and cumulatively harmful situation.

Another subtle means of ensuring that proper corrective action is taken is to require a copy of any report to be sent to the initiator's line manager or ultimate director. Responses to the report are subsequently circulated to those advised of the original incident or irregularity. It is also helpful for a section of the report document to carry the heading 'Steps taken to prevent a recurrence'.

To encourage the reporting of incidents or irregular-

ities, some companies offer an 'incentive scheme'
whereby employees are paid a percentage of any
savings, actual or potential, that can be attributed to
their action; alternatively, bonus points may be
awarded that can eventually be redeemed for goods.
Such a scheme may be appropriate to reward innova-
tion or cost savings, but it is of questionable value as an
inducement to discover fraud or malpractice because of
the obvious temptations of entrapment or deliberate
mistake.

For example, when it became known that credit card
companies were paying a reward to finders of credit
cards, service station operatives where credit card
transactions are high, were qualifying for several
rewards a week. Investigation showed suspiciously high
recoveries by certain employees, and several of the
'losers' were found to be friends of the 'finders'!

The company security adviser may stand in the
organisation's hierarchy below, say, the finance director or the company secretary, but his operational
reporting responsibility should be to the chief executive
so that he does not come up against political reserva-
tions or restrictions when he needs to do something in a
department whose head is more senior than his own.

Conflict of interests

To protect an employer against actual or potential
conflicts of interest, employees should be required, on
appointment and annually thereafter, to sign a declara-
tion that they have no interest, financial or otherwise,
in any company or individual with which the company
does business. Any other business involvement should
also be declared.

Internal audits

Functional audits performed by internal auditors and security surveys carried out by security staff on a regular basis should continually monitor, test and review laid down security procedures. These reviews should be included, where appropriate, in reports of security breaches which are circulated to the relevant line manager and the chief executive.

7   The Work of the Security Committee

Assessing the risk

One of the first tasks of a security committee must be to assess the risks to the continued profitable function of the organisation. A SWOT analysis (see p66) of the various line functions may be carried out.

It is imperative to question constantly just what it is that makes the company successful. The answer may be the superiority of the product, its reputation, its after-sales service, its price, its availability, its versatility or other factors in which it scores over its rivals.

Having identified the ingredients of success, it is crucial to establish what precisely gives the company its advantage over competitors. This is a difficult judgement to make requiring totally objective consideration. Longstanding members of the organisation may not be capable of the necessary objectivity, and this analysis might well be better conducted by a reputable management consultancy. Such a firm should at least be asked to provide someone well versed in the techniques of company evaluation to direct discussion amongst management in the most productive way.

If it is feared that the invitation of a stranger into the company may itself jeopardise security, an alternative approach is to enrol the various committee members for a course in management skills — including the functioning of committees. There are many business schools running very worthwhile courses of this kind.

Courses normally last several months and are invariably residential. Managers are taught to subordinate their functional skills and concentrate on developing good general managerial skills. Most managers are 'good at their job', that is the function that has probably got them to that position, but few have had any formal training in management itself, which is a quite distinct skill.

Once it is felt that the best possible managerial skills are represented on the committee, it is necessary to set a timetable for completing the various tasks before it. Nothing is more frustrating to members than plans and procedures that seem to drag on interminably.

Devising and operating a system of control

The next job of the committee is the preparation of company guidelines or a manual on security so that all personnel who receive a copy will know exactly what is required of them. Implicit in the guidelines is the idea that failure to comply would be a disciplinary offence within the company.

The manual should be designated 'Company Proprietary' and numbered copies should be issued personally to the departmental heads the committee has decided should receive it. Each volume must be signed for and given the sort of physical protection described in the next chapter.

The manual should lay down security procedures, including disaster planning (bomb threats, power cuts, machinery failure, acts of sabotage, etc), and set out a standard form in which all sorts of threats against the company's assets should be reported.

Security controls have to be exercised on people and by people, so they should not be so complex or illogical that they fall into disuse or abuse. All security measures have to be workable and acceptable to those required to operate them. There is no such thing as absolute security: the best systems, be they physical or procedural, can be broken with the right amount of skill, time and determination.

It is a good practice, fair to employer and employee alike, to put any critical procedures or practices into writing. Not only does this improve efficiency but it ensures that proper and uniform action is taken by all concerned. In addition it provides the sanction sometimes necessary if agreed (and notified) practices are ignored or circumvented.

There is nothing more frustrating for an auditor or investigator attempting to discover what went wrong and who was responsible for an irregularity to find that a document designed to show initials, date, time or other essential data is blank and that those who should have indicated their involvement with the transaction have omitted to do so. The excuses generally offered are that 'no-one bothers' or 'we never have the time'. The 'audit trail' should always be capable of identifying just who did what. Another benefit of ensuring that the part each person plays in a chain reaction is recorded on a document is that the more people put their signatures to that part of a transaction with which they are involved, the less chance there is of fraud. It is easier to acquiesce in a fraud if one does not have to sign a document knowing that it is incorrect.

Providing a reference document with a very high degree of physical security, using keys, combinations and passwords, may prove counter-productive. If several authorised persons have a frequent need for the document, even the best-intentioned will find a way of circumventing over-complicated procedures in an effort to get on with the job.

Certain geographical areas, processes or systems

within most organisations are defined as 'classified'. However open a company's management style may be, classified areas should be protected from access by all but those for whom it is essential.

The days are gone when anyone owning a computer would have it located on the ground floor, normally behind plate glass so that it could be seen from the street, and would take all visitors to see it. Computers have become critical to the functioning of many organisations, and they and their operators require the greatest physical protection.

8 Protecting the Areas of Risk

There are certain areas within a company to which unauthorised access must be prohibited. These should include research and development, the computer suite, the design studio and all other areas from which it is wise to exclude not only outsiders but also employees who do not have a need to go there.

Entrances and perimeter protection

Access control starts at the entrances to the premises. It is pointless to arrange good security procedures for the front door when there are other vulnerable points of entry. The back door needs particular attention if there is a loading/despatch bay through which access to the main part of the building can be gained. Personnel doors, fire exit doors and outside staircases need to be protected.

In a building which, to comply with fire regulations, has several perimeter fire exit doors, these are normally fitted with panic bars so that staff needing to leave in a hurry only have to lean on the bar to make the door open outwards immediately. Some occupiers prefer to lock or padlock these doors outside working hours; this is an acceptable, albeit a time-consuming practice, provided that no one is locked in, unable to get out safely in an emergency.

There are numerous devices on the market for these

doors, designed to give both safety and security. For the type of door that has to be unlocked or have a chain and padlock removed during occupancy, glass bolts should be fitted that prevent interference and present no trouble during an emergency exit since they shatter with pressure from the inside.

To make this kind of side door control more sophisticated each door can be fitted with a magnetic reed wired into the control unit so that it can be monitored at the security centre or reception; any attempt to open the door from the outside instantly identifies the location and activates a self-activating bell on the outside above the door.

Remember that a door that can be quickly opened at the side of a building can just as easily be deliberately left slightly open though apparently closed, to enable an outsider to gain unauthorised access.

A physical survey of the building should be conducted to identify all possible access points, including any vulnerable ground floor windows or possible access from adjoining buildings. An overall security plan should provide for a physically secure shell. Perimeter protection, as it is known, may also include an intruder alarm system to safeguard the building in times of non-occupancy.

Particularly sensitive buildings may be given additional protection by physical barriers of wire mesh fencing or pailings, by the use of movement detectors on the fences or set in the ground, or by infra-red beams across vulnerable expanses. All such systems would be monitored by a control unit secured within the perimeter protection; any alarm condition would be signalled silently by means of a dedicated telephone line to a central station which would be manned 24 hours a day and which would furnish the appropriate physical response to the sounding of the alarm.

Internal areas

Sensitive locations inside the perimeter can be given trap protection. That is, in addition to its built-in safety, a room, safe or cupboard can be protected by other means such as space or movement detectors relying on infra-red or passive infra-red rays or heat detectors. Internal doors can be contacted with magnetic reeds wired into the control unit and safes and cupboards can be additionally protected with magnetic devices whose alarm is set off by vibration in the event of an attempted forcing or from heat in the event of an attempted cutting or blowing by explosive.

There are ID card readers for use at the entry to such places: they allow access to authorised personnel and lock out all others. More sophisticated systems have a lock whose combination is known only to authorised personnel. There is an entry device which reads a finger or palm print and, in case there is an attempted forceful entry by duress, one system reads a retina print that is as distinctive as a finger print!

Access control of staff and visitors

Good physical security provides varying layers of security starting with the outside perimeter fence and continuing with the building itself and finally the trap-protected areas. These defences may force an intruder to conclude that the building would be more easily penetrated during day time occupancy.

Good access control is the only safeguard against this. Everybody entering the building, both staff and visitors must be channelled through one well-controlled access point, preferably manned by a full-time security guard. It is a false economy to ask a security guard to perform receptionist's duties as well as his security function. At times of great activity, for instance at start of work in the morning, or return from lunch hour, an intruder can easily mingle with a group of employees — even engaging one in conversation — and, if the guard is distracted by a duty other than pure security, the intruder will have got in undetected.

It has now become almost an essential requirement that staff are issued with ID cards with their photograph and signature heat-laminated into a plastic holder. For the maximum benefit of such a system all staff, however senior and well known, must be required to show their ID card to the security guard on entering the building, and notices to that effect should be displayed in the foyer or at the control point before access to lifts or staircases can be gained. The sensitivity of the building as a whole or certain parts of it will determine when staff need to display their ID cards.

The reluctance of staff to be photographed and give details for an ID card has been eroded in a world that progressively requires people to identify themselves. Once prepared and issued, the cards can be used as a means of identity in other company locations, on visits to suppliers and customers or for staff purchases, etc. Good enforcement makes the habit of showing an ID card as easy and acceptable as showing a season ticket to a railway inspector.

All visitors should be channelled securely to a reception point. The receptionist should contact the person to be visited to confirm the appointment. The visitor should then be escorted to the member of staff or collected by him to ensure that no visitor can get 'lost'. All visitors should, of course, be escorted off the premises on conclusion of their business.

If staff are required to show ID cards on entering the premises, it is essential that visitors are issued with temporary cards or visitors' badges to be worn all the time they are on the premises.

Many companies pay lip service to the idea of processing visitors and issuing temporary ID badges or cards, but few take the very basic and obvious steps needed to ensure that the system is foolproof. A bored receptionist will often ask somebody to sign the visitors' book and neglect to look at the entry. She will then issue a temporary pass saying, casually 'Don't forget to hand it in when you leave'. A temporary pass may give its owner limitless access to the building over an indefinite period of time. Many organisations are lax in their control and never receive back all the passes they issue. Some people keep them as souvenirs, some genuinely forget to return them but the professional spy may retain his to use again and again.

There is now on the market a 'self-destructing' temporary visitor's badge. It can be overprinted with the company's name, and the visitor's details can be inserted at the time of issue. The paper on which the badge is printed has been treated chemically so that while being worn under normal indoor lighting, the white background gradually changes to blue and, after some eight hours, the badge is completely unreadable. However, several minutes of exposure to outdoor light, even on an overcast day, causes the entire background to turn blue, making the badge useless. The badges come in sheets of 12, conveniently mounted on a board. As each one is completed, a duplicate copy remains on the board so that subsequent control is a simple matter. The problem of collecting returned badges is solved since once they have discoloured they are of no further use. Staff should be encouraged to challenge anybody wearing a dark blue visitor's badge!

Files

Many employees may require facilities for properly securing things of importance. The security survey or the security committee should identify sensitive items and materials and provide the means of securing them.

Offices that contain files on personnel, marketing strategy, wage negotiations, research and development and anything else that may be deemed classified must be equipped with safes or good quality steel presses so that staff have the ability — and the explicit duty — to lock away such material when not actually in use.

Specialist advice should be obtained on the most suitable type of safe. Fire resistance could be an advantage where protection is required both against theft and destruction. It should also be remembered that safes are frequently vulnerable because they are not set into concrete or bolted and/or grouted into surrounding brickwork, and they are sometimes carried away intact by thieves to be worked on under better conditions.

Steel presses normally have a simple push button lock at the top which is not very difficult to pick. Their security should be enhanced with a solid vertical locking bar passing through all the door handles and welded top and bottom to the frame, secured with a good quality lever padlock or combination lock.

The combination for a lock should never be written on the back of the cabinet, or on a piece of paper stuck in the pin tray of the nearest desk. These are the first places an industrial spy would look! Nor should a combination which is easily guessed such as 00000, 12345 or one's date of birth be used. It should not be too difficult to think of a number that has some association with the user so that it can be remembered without being written down anywhere. If recording it is absolutely essential it should be done in a personal diary in such a way that only the writer can tell what it is.

The locks supplied on most office desk drawers are scarcely a deterrent since they can be opened with a letter opener. Even if they are secure it is not too difficult to remove desk drawers either from underneath or through the back of a desk. In the main desk drawers are unsuitable for storage of sensitive material.

In an office which has secure lockable filing cabinets and presses these should be used to secure sensitive papers during any absence from the office — to lunch, coffee or even the toilet! It is a good idea to make a large sign to place on the cabinet when you open it: 'FILING CASE OPEN'. Then each time you leave the office a quick glance around will tell you that you need to lock up before you go. This routine not only reduces the risk of files being stolen or looked at by a spy or unauthorised employee, but also prevents the tiresome 'borrowing' of a file or document by colleagues without permission.

Security classification system

The first necessity to determine the level of security appropriate for a document is to decide what is confidential and what is not.

The security committee may decide that there should be, say, three levels of security classification within the company: unclassified (the overwhelming majority), private or restricted (matters pertaining to personnel, pay and conditions, union negotiations, price structures), and secret or company proprietary (the unauthorised disclosure of which would have a serious effect on the company).

The classification of a document should always be the

responsibility of the originator as indeed should be the distribution list. It is a good security (and business) practice to ensure that the distribution of sensitive documents is no more than absolutely essential; the determining factor is a 'need to know'. Many originators of sensitive material are tempted to let too many people see it because they are so proud of it. But this is dangerous from a security point of view because every additional copy requires special handling and storage treatment.

Another tendency which should be guarded against is to give one's work too high a security classification. Originators or their line managers must try to be objective so as to ensure that the system is not overloaded.

It is equally important to review classified material regularly, and to down-grade it when it is no longer secret or company proprietary.

Transmission of documents

A document should bear its security classification together with its originator's details. When being despatched by company internal mail it should be placed in an envelope addressed to the individual concerned, possibly stamped with the instruction 'To be opened by addressee only' and marked with the originator's details in case some other person in the addressee's office has reason to contact the originator. This envelope should then be placed inside another envelope addressed to the recipient's office, bearing no reference to the security classification recorded on the inner envelope.

It enhances security (and saves on stationery) if the outer is a used one so that a cursory examination of mail in transit gives no obvious evidence of what may be classified. Many companies have inter-office correspondence envelopes with printed provision for several destinations which are crossed through when the next is added. These are ideal for containing other envelopes actually enclosing security classified documents. The outer envelope should be sealed with the sort of gummed paper that is moistened by a water wheel so that the originator can sign over the sealing tape and envelope to prevent unauthorised interference.

Mail rooms may need special security procedures. X-ray machines may be used to detect explosive devices if the organisation is a possible target for this kind of attack. There may also be a need for accounting controls if envelopes containing cash or cheques are opened in the mail room.

A procedure for dealing with mail which is merely addressed to the company should be laid down. If it is opened in the mail room and directed to the proper person or department, the person in charge of the mail room should be a responsible and preferably a senior member of staff who can judge whether something opened is likely to be classified and warrants the double envelope treatment.

Photocopiers

Most photocopying machines installed in offices are rented from one of the major suppliers; users pay a fixed rental with a surcharge dependent on the number of copies produced. Photocopies are expensive, but with so many machines available, there is a tendency to use them much more than is necessary. (Most companies have also to bear the inevitable unauthorised private use by employees.)

Photocopiers are an ever-present threat to security, particularly if they are available for free use by anyone in the vicinity, but certain modifications and controls will ensure that abuses and risks are kept to a minimum.

For example, photocopiers located on different floors of a building can each be fitted with a device that clearly marks the floor number on every sheet of copying paper in such a way that it cannot be erased but not so noticeably that it obscures any of the text copied. This will not stop unauthorised copying but it will at least ensure that any unauthorised copies that subsequently come to light can be traced back to their source. A similar control technique is to have a coloured prism or filter incorporated in the machine, or a particular pattern or etching, to identify the source of a photocopy. Coloured toners can also be employed in the different machines and a code devised, such as red for financial, blue for personnel, green for marketing, etc.

Any or all of the above procedures will assist in identifying the source of a copy document, indicating either where it was produced or whose original was used. More effective security can be provided by physical controls on the machine.

Ideally, photocopying machines should be under the control of a member of the stationery department or company administration to ensure proper use of the equipment. The power source should always be locked off when the machine is unsupervised.

If a permanent attendant is not feasible, lockable machines should be provided with only authorised persons holding keys. A log should be provided and a reconciliation should be conducted by an independent person at reasonable frequency to agree key counter readings with the log. Any apparent over-use should be taken up with the individual's line manager.

Copies of sensitive documents should each be numbered and perhaps bear some distinctive marking or
code identifying their source. Of course, this type of
control only helps to identify the source of a leak *after
the event.*

Ensuring that a sensitive document is not copied
anywhere is a problem to which there is no commercial-
ly acceptable solution as yet. One photocopying supplier has successfully produced a burgundy paper
which, when exposed to the intensity of light that
photocopiers use, turns black, rendering what was on
the original completely illegible. However, the cost of
the burgundy paper is prohibitive and is unlikely for the
time being to be used, except in certain government or
military situations.

Typewriters

After use on a sensitive document 'one shot' ribbons
should be incinerated or otherwise effectively destroyed since it is possible to read what was typed from
them. In an area where most of what is produced on
such a typewriter is sensitive, the machine should be
locked away when not in use to protect what would be
readable from a partly used spool.

Repairmen and contract workers

All visitors, including regular ones such as office and
equipment cleaners and service engineers must be
checked by security and issued with an ID card. It is
usually possible to arrange with a contractor that he will
continue to send the same individuals to a job, so that

checks can be made on background and work performance.

Certain work areas or equipment may be so sensitive
that any maintenance work will have to be supervised
by an established member of staff. This applies
particularly to cleaners who normally work early in the
morning or late in the evening so as not to interfere
with the normal work.

Random checks should be made on staff whose job it
is to supervise contract workers. Familiarity often leads
to a situation in which the supervisor 'leaves the
contractor to it' and goes off to have a coffee or read
the paper. When a security guard is given this kind of
duty, the supervision frequently tends to deteriorate to
the point where if a contractor needs to gain access to a
sensitive area the guard may just hand over the key,
asking for it to be returned on completion of the job!
Random checks and disciplinary action where necessary, are probably the most effective ways of dealing
with this very common problem.

Counterfeiting

One difficulty frequently encountered by investigators
attempting to prove that a product has been copied,
and subsequently marketed by a pirate manufacturer, is
positive identification of the genuine article. If the case
is brought to court it must rely on absolute proof.

There is a product on the market to deal with this
problem. It is a coated paper that incorporates an
ultra-violet activated 'watermark' in the form of the
required trade mark or logo. The paper costs less than
traditional watermarked paper and the coding can be
incorporated into product packaging, labelling, instruction books, guarantees and so on; it can cope with all

types of printing techniques – litho, letterpress, gravure, etc; and it can be supplied with pressure sensitive adhesive or gummed coating on the reverse. The process can be applied to paper or board, on any colour-tinted surface as well as white.

The process has many applications including diplomas, membership cards, ID cards, product labels, cheques, bonds, certificates, admission tickets, National Identity cards, birth certificates, bank notes, packaging, etc.

To determine whether a product is genuine or not only requires the simple test of exposing the article to a long or short wave ultra-violet light source. The device used for this can be pocket size so that a company's own sales force can easily check the authenticity of products on retailers' shelves. If a further and more conclusive test is required, a simple chemical solution can be applied to bring up the 'hidden' code.

The knowledge that genuine products have been treated in this way may, itself, deter the industrial spy from stealing the idea in the first place.

9 Security Procedures and Equipment

Board room security

Probably the most sensitive and therefore vulnerable area in any company is the board room where the critical decisions involving the organisation are taken.

It should ideally be located at the top and within the heart of the building, certainly within the trap-protected area. It should always be kept locked when not in use and a procedure should be instituted whereby any repairman, contractor or other visitor who needs to enter the room is accompanied and supervised throughout.

If the board room has windows that can be over-looked, these should be protected with curtains and venetian blinds to prevent laser beams monitoring conversations.

Lifts and staircases giving access to the board room should be capable of being locked off to prevent unauthorised access not only during meetings but at times of non-occupancy.

If access control along a corridor leading to the board room is considered desirable it may be worth installing closed circuit television with a monitor in the security centre or guard location.

No telephones should be necessary in the board room, and if telephones have been taken out or disconnected it should be realised that any wires or conduits which remain behind could be used by someone installing listening devices. Wires supplying electricity are just as vulnerable in this respect. Board rooms need to be searched frequently, both by physical search and electronic means, and especially *immediately* before a meeting. The physical search must include a thorough examination of every article in the room − table, chairs, light fittings, desk equipment, pictures; walls also need to be examined carefully. A skilled and experienced searcher will look for the unusual in the usual, for evidence of disturbance in quality or colour, and even for dust distribution which may give an indication of interference.

This type of physical search must be augmented by an electronic sweep or search. There are numerous systems on the market which claim to be able to detect devices used by industrial spies. The competence − and the price − of detection systems varies greatly from one manufacturer to another. So confident of successful detection is one manufacturer that he guarantees a full cash refund for the detection system (some £19,000) if the user does not find at least one hidden eavesdropping bug within the first 60 days of use! If an electronic sweep is to be undertaken it should be as effective as possible, and there is a system which can detect dormant devices of the type only activated by voice or a particular signal, as well as those that are always live.

It may be worthwhile changing the date and time of an extremely sensitive meeting by word of mouth just before it is scheduled to be held. An alternative scheme would be to change the venue at the last moment to a conference room or hotel suite that had not earlier been used for such a purpose. Thorough screening would need to be conducted by security personnel before such a proposed meeting, and the venue should also have been 'vetted' beforehand by security.

Telecommunications

All forms of communication which use public telephone wires or a public electricity supply are vulnerable to attack.

Telephones

In view of the large number of devices that can be employed to tap telephones and the wide range of situations in which they can be utilised, ie the instrument itself, its wires, junction boxes, main frames, private and public exchanges, telephone poles, etc, it is prudent to assume that no telephone is a safe means of private conversation.

Apart from the possibility of deliberate interference, the frequency with which one can get a crossed line in the normal course of events should make one circumspect when transmitting secret information by phone.

It is a matter of skill and self-discipline to conduct a conversation as if the call were being monitored by a third party. The subject being discussed can be protected by the use of inference or 'code talk' which is only understood by the two participants in the conversation.

It is worth taking a leaf out of any professional villain's book. He will always assume that his telephone is being intercepted by the authorities; he will use a bewildering mixture of slang and strange words (almost a foreign language) and will always refer to the 'things', without specifying what they are since the other party should know, and indicate places without naming them (eg 'where we met Benny last week'). For the greatest security a telephone is used just to arrange a meeting in a place where the conversation can take place in complete privacy.

However, for certain high level security purposes, scrambling devices can be fitted to telephones. The two parties are equipped with 'opposite ends' of the device and can communicate safely with each other, secure in the knowledge that any monitoring equipment will pick up only an incomprehensible noise.

Telexes

Telex communications are vulnerable in the same ways as telephonic ones. Organisations which need to send frequent messages of a sensitive nature should devise their own code. If the contents of the messages are basically repetitive they can easily be reduced to just the variables. This not only gives security, it also lowers the cost of telexing by reducing the amount of text.

For example, a regular transmitter of confidential commodity prices may need to send:

> Gold base 230   index + 4
> Silver base 212   index − 10
> Cocoa base 64   index + 7
> Coffee base 102   index − 3

A code agreed between the sender and receiver could reduce the various commodities to one alphabetical letter (not, of course, readily identifiable). Gold might be *a*; Silver, *g*; Cocoa, *l*; Coffee, *y*, and so on. As the words 'base' and 'index' are common in every instance they need not be transmitted. So, using another single code to express the numbers as letters, with a plus or minus sign merely being transmitted as *p* or *m*, the above message would become:

> *a,ltv,pg*
> *g,lal,mav*
> *l,xg,pc*
> *y,avl,mt*

By devising code 'dictionaries' for phrases typically and repeatedly used, messages involving more written text than numerical data may be treated similarly. For example:

> Vessel *A* sailed Halifax 0700 in ballast
> Estimated New York 21 February loading
> 500 tons machinery spares, 40 cars deck cargo
> Sailing 23 for Brest

The code might be: Vessel *A* = *XYGA;* sailed = *LRTG;* Halifax = *BTNO;* in ballast = *PRLD;* estimated = *TRDA;* and so on. With the numbers, since they would have no apparent significance in the midst of four letter code groups, becoming simply 1 = *A*, 2 = *B*, 3 = *C*, 0700 = *JGJJ*, etc, the message would read:

> *XYGA LRTG BTNO JGJJ PRLD*
> *TRDA* ....

Such a system is relatively secure, and once a matched pair of code books has been produced, the actual encoding and decoding of messages is quite simple.

A more secure code requires the initial transmission of a coded key which enables the recipient to set up the appropriate key to decode, followed by a transposition of letters in a particular pattern that cannot be translated to plain language until and unless the correct key is set up and the actual transposition code held. This system is best used by dividing the plain text into, say, five letter groups, irrespective of natural breaks between words, starting in the middle of the text, ending it with the word BISECT, before carrying on to the beginning of the message. For example, a typical message prepared for encoding:

> The market is expected / to rise to an all time high
> by Friday close of business

would read:

***RVRLE TORIS ETOAN ALLTI MEHIG
HBYFR IDAYC LOSEO FBUSI NESSB
ISECT THEMA RKETI SEXPE CTEDZ+**

*indicates code used and setting
+odd obvious letter to make up five letter group

Teleprinters can also use the Murray Code. This
expresses all the letters of the alphabet by different
combinations of holes punched over and below a line
on a tape. It can be made more secure by running a
simultaneous continuous coded tape (a duplicate of
which the recipient runs) so that the message is only
comprehensible at the encoding and decoding teleprinters.

It should be added that some postal authorities
refuse to relay coded messages that they are unable to
understand on grounds of national security. Most
authorities will refuse to transmit groups which contain
both letters and figures. However, it should be possible
to get round this by offering the authorities the key to
the code and ensuring that the encoded groups are
either letters or numbers, not mixed!

From a cost point of view coded messages are
effective. A five-letter group is charged as 'one word',
so there is a clear advantage over plain text messages in
this respect. For example;

Thank you for your letter of 4th January and I am
most interested to learn that you are producing a book

– charged 21 words

**THANK YOUFO RYOUR LETTE ROFFO
URTHJ ANUAR YANDI AMMOS TINTE
RESTE DTOLE ARNTH ATYOU AREPR
ODUCI NGABO OKZAZ**

– charged 18 words

Only really sensitive traffic needs this treatment, the vast bulk of messages transmitted by teleprinter being of an unclassified nature.

Security checks

As we have said, security systems and procedures, however well devised, are only as good as the people who operate them. Thorough checks, carried out at random intervals, are the only way to ensure that the maximum possible security is being maintained.

A particularly effective way of raising security awareness is for someone to make a tour of a sensitive area during lunch time or after working hours, taking anything of proprietary or intrinsic value (such as calculators or valuable personal effects) which has been left unsecured, leaving a note that the article(s) can be collected from the individual's line manager! The check should include security of safes, cabinets, steel presses, desk drawers, etc. Such an exercise needs to be carried out with care: some of the offenders may well be senior staff who do not take too kindly to activities like this. However, if the activity is sanctioned by the chief executive or the security committee it should be seen to be to the benefit of all — either in helping to protect the livelihood of everyone in the company, or in avoiding thefts of wallets and purses, etc which create an atmosphere of inevitable suspicions and misgivings.

Intruder alarm systems

Alarm systems should be tested from time to time. A 'dry run' tests not only the system but also those concerned with its operation.

The operation of some detectors can be monitored by the control unit. To avoid wasting police time when the silent autodial alarm is to be tested, it is essential to give the central station details of the exercise by a pre-arranged telephone message, taking care to inform them of the completion time as well as the starting time so that a subsequent real attack is not ignored.

It might also be worthwhile to test the call-out time of listed keyholders to the premises in the event that the central station receives an alarm signal.

Shredders and waste disposal

All organisations engaged in sensitive work should possess at least one effective shredder to destroy confidential waste.

Most of the small shredders that operate moving teeth are prone to jamming or occasionally let through a large piece. The jamming creates a fire risk, the large unshredded pieces a security risk. Moreover, the strips of waste produced can be pieced together and read, especially if the paper has been fed through in the direction of print and not against it.

The best machine is a disintegrator which is capable of swallowing bound manuals, crumpled paper, unburst computer printout, microfiche – reel and all, offset plates, rolled maps, blue prints, printed circuit boards, and carbon – including needles, syringes, plastic and glass. It reduces everything to 'confetti'. One disintegrator on the market has a built-in vacuum system which eliminates dust and automatically collects and prepares material for easy disposal in a form ten times more compact than that produced by the less efficient shredders. Several different sized models are available. If the size of the waste problem does not justify having full-time use of such equipment, securable confidential waste bags can be provided where necessary which should be kept locked away and collected when there is enough for a worthwhile 'run' on the disintegrator. The collection and disposal of this waste should not be left to contract cleaners but should be a properly supervised security operation.

There are also security companies that offer a specialised security waste disposal service. Confidential waste is collected by their vehicles; a receipt is given for the number of sealed bags; and a certificate of disposal is subsequently issued. Users of such a service are recommended occasionally to observe in a covert way a typical run to satisfy themselves that they are getting what they pay for. Several unfortunate cases have recently come to light in which confidential medical records and even police files have been discovered on public refuse tips.

Not all confidential waste disposal companies are reliable. The value of scrap paper, particularly computer-produced stationery, may tempt a dishonest employee to make a private arrangement with a scrap paper merchant. The issue of a certificate of destruction is then meaningless. It is obvious, therefore, that risks are considerably reduced by effective destruction carried out in-house.

10 Staff Selection and Training

Recruitment

Most companies employ their own specialists in recruitment. The personnel or employee relations department, having obtained the necessary approval for the post, may assist the individual or department wishing to appoint someone to produce a 'profile' for the job. Qualifications, age range, experience and scope of the job offered are matters for the department concerned, while personnel will advise on the salary range and benefits.

The latter may well be based on information gained from surveys conducted amongst similar companies. It is not unusual for major companies to co-operate freely in exchanges of this sort of information. All companies to a greater or lesser extent have various levels of recruitment and scales or salary bands within those levels, and it is mutually beneficial that company A offers the same sort of pay and conditions for, say, a chemical engineer graduate as company B.

Broad levels of recruitment could be unskilled, semi-skilled, professional or graduate. The last level is the most critical to the company's continuing success because today's recruits have the chance of being in the very highest posts tomorrow. Recognising the importance of graduate recruitment, many companies seek to recruit directly from universities before the results of the final exams are known. Experienced personnel staff build up contacts within universities and are able to make reasonable assessments of students. They then offer jobs to those who appear to have the best potential conditional upon exam results. Even in a depressed recruitment market there is still intense competition to have the pick of the bunch.

For other appointments, companies may choose to employ the services of agencies who specialise in the particular field of expertise sought.

Whatever method of recruitment is chosen the search for the right candidate requires considerable effort and may also be expensive. Once funds have been made available for the appointment, there is often a tendency to hurry the process of selection. This is extremely dangerous because appointing the wrong person to a key post can be a very costly business for the company. Once the appointment has been taken up, recognising that the person is not right for the job may be hard, and then there are the complications and costs of getting rid of the person and starting the whole process of recruitment again. From the security point of view, it is alarming for the company to have opened its doors and its files to somebody in these circumstances.

Mistakes in recruitment often arise not through lack of knowledge or experience but through a failure to ensure that the company is getting the person it thinks it is *before the job offer is made*. It is an essential part of recruitment that background checks are made and satisfactorily concluded before any commitment is made.

Medical

Whatever the qualifications, experience or age of the candidate chosen, the employer needs to be satisfied that his general health is such that he will be capable of carrying out his duties without excessive absences or the need for surgery which might impair his future health or efficiency. If the company does not have its own medical adviser to conduct this investigation an outside medical consultant should be engaged.

It is also normal to ask applicants to complete and sign a questionnaire which requires the disclosure of certain illnesses, operations and conditions. The questionnaire should include a clause to the effect that failure to disclose relevant information or making deliberately false replies to the questions could render the person liable to instant dismissal. It should also authorise the company to make inquiries to verify the stated facts.

Like insurance companies an applicant may not be debarred because of a disclosed medical problem, but the employer (like an insurance company) is entitled to know the risk he is taking and make a decision in the light of the facts. It is manifestly unfair to have to judge a situation after it has arisen particularly when earlier disclosure may have given the opportunity for a different decision at that time.

So that a person's medical history can be properly researched and advised upon, it is essential that the medical practitioner whose job it is to advise, is given sufficient time if necessary to seek advice of the applicant's general practitioner and allow for any follow-up medical tests, x-rays or investigations.

To allow the employer the maximum protection; provided that the medical practitioner has been given sufficient time and facilities to complete his investigations and examinations properly, there would be a greater chance of successfully suing him if there was subsequent evidence of professional incompetence, an eventuality for which medical practitioners are required to be insured against.

Pre-employment vetting

At some stage in the recruitment process, candidates are required to complete an application for employment form, usually designed by the company. It will require the basic information that identifies the person: full name, date and place of birth, nationality, current address, professional and academic qualifications. There may also be sections dealing with the specific job.

For recruitment to a senior position it is prudent to ask for home addresses over the past ten years and the entire employment history (including military service), listing full names and addresses of previous employers, job titles, dates of employment and reasons for leaving. The form should ask for all schools, colleges and universities to be listed with dates and qualifications gained. Three references, either personal or professional, should also be required.

Photocopies of certificates, diplomas or degrees should not in any circumstances be acceptable because of the high incidence of forgeries. The originals should always be inspected, their details should be abstracted for verification and they should then be returned to the applicant.

The application for employment should end with the requirement of truthful disclosure and an authorisation to the company to verify the stated particulars. Such a clause, which would be subject to advice from the company's legal adviser, may take a form such as:

> In connection with this application for employment I authorise all corporations, companies, credit agencies, educational institutions, persons, law enforcement agencies, former employers and the military services to release information they may have about me to the person or company with

which this application has been filed and release them from any liability and responsibility from doing so.

The value of asking for personal references may be questioned. Who, in his right mind, would ever give as a reference someone he thought would speak ill of him? However, if references are requested they should be properly taken up by someone trained to get the best out of them.

Too many companies send 'standard letters' to referees which at best tend to elicit 'standard replies'. Most are never replied to for many reasons, not the least of which is a reluctance to put in writing anything derogatory about a previous employee that could result in action. To attempt to frame simple questions on such a letter requiring a yes/no answer is rarely useful. The very minimum requirement is for the person conducting the pre-employment vetting to speak to the referee on the telephone, but it is much better to arrange an interview in which more information is likely to be forthcoming.

Verifying curricula vitae

There are so many pitfalls in verifying curricula vitae. If it cannot be done adequately, many believe it is better not to do it at all. But if the company has the time and skills to do a thorough and professional job, it can avoid a great deal of harm, financial loss and suffering that can result from a wrong decision.

Pre-employment vetting is emphatically not a job for personnel or employee relations department. Not only is their training and expertise inappropriate – they have different criteria by which to evaluate an applicant and different goals. Indeed, their involvement in pre-employment vetting is as undesirable as the 'information gathering organisation' (CIA) being allowed executive power and acting on it in the Bay of Pigs incident referred to in Chapter 1. If the applicant is hired, the knowledge of his background which someone in personnel may have gained could cause mistrust or discomfort to their party. This is one reason for vetting being carried out by an organisation that does not need to have a continuing relationship with the individual should he become a regular employee.

Another reason for those who have been involved in the selection procedure not to do the vetting themselves is that they may find themselves in a conflict of interest situation. Effective vetting requires training, experience and the skills of an investigator; impartiality is extremely important.

The most effective pre-employment vetting is done by the employer's own professional investigative staff, which smaller companies will not be able to afford. The best alternative to this is to use a specialist agency with investigators who are skilled at interviewing people and exercising judgement and who know where to research information and how to gain access to records not normally considered available to the public.

A thorough pre-employment vetting will start with proving the applicant's birth or, certainly, his date of birth. It is a well known subterfuge to change the year of birth to one either side of the truth (ie to use 1934 or 1936 instead of 1935) or to transpose date and month (ie 6/5 − 6 May instead of 5/6 − 5 June). Either or both devices could well make checks in criminal records useless as these invariably identify by date of birth. Luckily for the applicant, such a small 'error' can, if detected, convincingly be explained as a typing error.

Similar 'confusion' can be caused on a handwritten form. A 3 can be written to look like an 8, a 2 might look like a 7, or vice versa. This is a useful trick used in trying to gain or lose five years' work at retirement, or to qualify for a job that specifies an upper or lower age limit.

Professional and educational qualifications are frequently 'bought' and even more frequently forged. Only proper checking procedures can establish which qualifications are genuine.

Gaps in employment dates or claims to have worked for a company now in liquidation or as a self-employed consultant from a home address may all be too difficult for someone not trained as an investigator to check, and they may be the very indication of the applicant's attempt to cover up something he does not want a prospective employer to know. Elaborating a job description or exaggerating a previous salary is dishonest, but 'stretching' start and finish dates for previous employment may be much more sinister. A prospective employer needs to know the facts established by a competent impartial investigator before he can decide if a discovered 'error' was malicious or unintentional or insignificant.

A recent case of failure adequately to check the background of a City of San Francisco official revealed after he had resigned that:

1. He had given as his home address and phone number, the number and address of another person (later convicted of crime).

2. He had lied about his education claiming he had attended L'Ecole Hotelière in Lausanne, Switzerland; Cornell University School of Hotel Administration and Purdue. Far from being the honours graduate he claimed to be, he never attended the Swiss school or Cornell and had only taken a one day $65 cost control management course in San Diego.

3. He had omitted from his application the fact that he had owned and operated a Las Vegas restaurant that had closed four months after opening and another in Carmel, California that failed resulting in a number of law suits.
4. He failed to mention that he had worked as a floorman in a Vegas casino where he had given his true birth date of 1934; on his application form he had given 1935.

The case involving Janet Cooke, the reporter on the *Washington Post* who won a Pulitzer Prize on the basis of a trumped up story, is even better known. Later investigations showed that the 'credentials' that got her the job in the first instance had been falsified.

The fundamental function of all investigators is to check declared facts; and they must have the means to do so.

It is just as important to be able to verify something as it is to disprove it. Pre-employment checks are by no means all negative. Vetting established employees, either at times when a significant promotion is contemplated or at reasonable intervals, is a good practice. It should apply to all levels of senior staff: it helps to prevent discontent if it can be seen that nobody is made an exception, and the company can be reassured that, for instance, the person recruited as an accountant ten years ago, who is now financial director, is still the person he was that long ago.

What sympathy can a court be expected to extend to a company whose funds have been embezzled by a cashier who had previous convictions for the same offence which would have come to light if pre-employment vetting had taken place? What defence against an action for negligence would an employer have if a new employee molested women in his office if it could be shown that that kind of behaviour was the reason for dismissal from his previous job?

The facts are there to be proved or disproved. The job needs to be done properly. The recruitment time may be the only time when both sides have to be completely frank with each other. Once an employee is 'on the payroll' it is always much more difficult to get him off it!

Good recruitment means not hiring until you are sure of your facts. Time must be allowed for medical examinations and pre-employment vetting to be carried out properly. As New York's largest pre-employment screening organisation has it: 'Your judgement is no better than your information.'

Training

It is generally accepted that a company's employees are its most valuable assets. Not only should they be protected by the sort of physical and procedural security systems described earlier, but their value should be enhanced by further training and development, either in-house or on outside courses.

Training in the particular skills required to do the job is obviously important, and the ways in which it can be done will easily suggest themselves. Training in the skills of management requires more consideration.

In many large companies in-house training of individuals from different disciplines and of varying age and experience in management principles achieves good results. But many feel that the most effective training in making decisions and achieving objectives is through simulation and role-playing, and this type of training is usually more successful when conducted on a residential basis by an outside consultancy. Not only is concentration improved when trainees are away from their normal environment and responsibilities, but participants feel more free to find their own level of performance than they do when training within the company with their senior colleagues. Role-playing is much more difficult when everyone knows everyone else.

Training has a particularly important function in the open and participative management style which organisations are increasingly adopting. It is a basic way of securing and maintaining the loyalty of employees. In the absence of training, advice or just plain information about the company's methods and plans suspicion and mistrust flourish, and security is threatened by the consequent lack of loyalty amongst the staff.

Many companies run induction courses for all new employees to give them an overall picture of what the company does and how it does it. This ensures that individuals who have been recruited to do a specialised job know what others around them are doing and how they all interact with each other. This is an ideal occasion for the security adviser to be introduced. His department will in any case probably be involved at an early stage when ID cards are prepared and issued. Employees are at their most receptive when they start a job, so the induction course is an excellent opportunity to make them security conscious.

11 Computer Security

Physical security

When deciding on a location for the computer suite, one needs to take into account its vulnerability to unlawful intrusion and the risks of damage or destruction by fire or flood.

The ground floor or basement of a building may be the best place to accommodate the sometimes heavy equipment if, in the building stage, attention is paid to protection against fire and flood. One major hazard might be flooding when a fire occurs on a floor above and the large quantity of water used to extinguish it finds its way into the computer suite. A very slight slope in the floor is an excellent protection against damage by flood as the water will drain away much faster than from a flat floor. The suite should have fire-cladding insulation.

A tailor-made computer suite would probably be a shell capsule, like a box with top and bottom to the sides, capable in itself of accommodating and supporting the equipment, personnel and ancillaries necessary to support the operation, set inside the building.

Since the power supply and air conditioning plant are vital to the uninterrupted operation of the computer suite, there must be a contingency plan to provide alternatives in the event of a power failure or other major malfunction.

Power cables are channelled in trunking across the bottom of a computer suite, normally under a 'false' floor to allow easy access if the need arises. They must not be under the lower part of a sloping floor where water could collect.

The air conditioning plant should have its inlet physically protected so that noxious substances or gases cannot be ingested, and the outlet should be protected so that it cannot be blocked — accidentally or deliberately.

Access control is of paramount importance to any computer centre and a high security system must be installed such as ID cards specially coded for use with a card reader at the entrance. If the entrance door is the type that spring-closes extra supervision is needed to make sure that only the authorised person is admitted, and to make sure that there is no interference with the closing mechanism by wedging the door open or disconnecting the spring or plunger.

There is much to commend an access system which, although obviously more expensive, prints out a timed record of personnel entering and leaving a particular area; it is operated by the feeding of the ID card into the card reader. Cards which have been withdrawn or reported lost or stolen can be 'locked out' in such a system, and any attempt to use one can be signalled covertly.

Back-up and library tapes need to be stored securely in another location so that in the event of a disaster in the operational suite, all is not lost. The security committee will have a contingency plan for the use of equipment in another company or building.

If only one operator is required to be on duty during silent hours, close-circuit television should be installed with a monitor in the security guard's office or other 24-hour manned location so that an accident or sudden illness can be spotted immediately.

No personnel working in the computer centre should be allowed to take handbags, briefcases, etc into the actual workplace. This not only makes it difficult to remove a disc or tape from the centre without authorisation; it also helps to prevent the possibility of a disgruntled employee bringing in a powerful magnet to destroy electromagnetic data. Computer personnel should not be allowed to take refreshment at their place of work because of the risk of food or drink accidentally being spilt into the equipment. A rest room provided with personal lockers near the working area will make restrictions such as these quite acceptable to staff.

Personnel

In-depth pre-employment screening is recommended for all personnel within the computer facility. They work in the very heart of the organisation, and with the right skills and determination the computer offers limitless scope for fraud. A second reason for exercising special care in recruitment of computer personnel is that they have a tendency to be nomadic, staying only a short time with each employer.

Since computer technology and the language attached to it are relatively new, employers and their personnel departments often do not know what to expect of staff. Computer qualifications, unlike those of a botanist, engineer or chemist, are quite new — as are some of the colleges and universities offering them. Computer jargon almost constitutes a foreign language, but the employer must not make the mistake of abrogating all responsibility for the computer and its operatives, leaving it all to 'those who understand it'. The employer who acts in this way leaves himself very vulnerable, and he must think of the computer as only another business tool, and those responsible for its operation as merely technically qualified staff.

Even within the computer centre, some programs are so sensitive as to require additional protection to ensure that only those few personnel authorised to access them can do so. This can either be physical, that is, the tapes of programs are secured by good quality lock or combination locks and/or they can only be accessed by the use of a secret password or code.

Such sensitive data would obviously include payroll details and possibly discount levels and to whom they applied. If not properly protected and monitored, the latter kind of program can present a great opportunity to the dishonest operator to collude with the customer, raising discount levels to their mutual financial benefit.

'Hackers'

Events have occurred recently in the USA which should serve as a warning to us all.

In the USA there is a growing band of youngsters, brought up on science fiction stories and films, exposed to computer toys and games from early childhood and taught in school how to operate computers. These young people have become known as 'hackers'.

The object of their game is to gain access to protected programs, not only in industry but also in government and even in the Department of Defence. By various subterfuges on the telephone, they learn the appropriate code or password. One hacker recently admitted in a television interview that one of the simplest ways to learn a secret code was to telephone someone in the target organisation and say: 'Look, I've only just started here in the EDP centre and I need to know the password for the XYZ program but I can't find my supervisor. Can you tell me what it is?' People are usually so naturally helpful that the information is frequently given without difficulty!

In one recent case, a hacker who had gained unauthorised access to numerous privileged programs used his 'skills' with devastating effect. Whenever he was 'cut up' by another car on the road, he would use the licensing computer to ascertain the owner's name and address. Armed with that information he would access the hire purchase company's computer and insert data to the effect that the owner was behind with his payments and that instant repossession was required. He would cancel the driver's insurance policy, make false entries of traffic violations in the police computer such that the next time the driver was checked by police he would be arrested and bail would not be granted. He would cancel the driver's credit cards and have his telephone cut off.

One young group of hackers managed successfully to penetrate the systems of an engineering college, a Los Angeles bank and a cancer centre, and one or two of them then went on to infiltrate the Los Alamos nuclear weapons laboratory system.

Although some, including the *Washington Post*, have likened such escapades to those of their predecessors the 'phone freaks', dismissing the whole matter as nothing more than the highjinks of high-spirited youngsters, it is an extremely serious security problem.

Word processors

Information is stored on floppy diskettes or hard disks for use with a word processor in much the same way as such information is stored in computer systems, making unauthorised access to or interference with the information a real risk.

Certain word processors offer as an additional

security protection procedure a memory component in the system master and peripherals which eliminates data from these devices as soon as they are powered off and which can be combined with the availability of fully removable media. This technique the manufacturer refers to as a hardware security feature and means that the disks can and should be physically removed and stored in good quality security cabinets.

A more advanced system, in addition to the above, has password protection, described as a software ancillary, and the facility to erase a document or volume by overwriting the text three times and verifying the overwriting process at each pass.

Password protection is, of itself, a further refinement to a 'log-on' feature and both codes need to be entered to obtain access to the most sensitive material.

Although the password is suppressed as it is entered, that is it is not displayed on the screen, it has to be the unique creation of the user. It must be memorable: to write it down anywhere would defeat the object of the exercise. It can happen that a user selects a word which is predictable to a third party, such as a partner's name or the name of a pet.

Manufacturers of password protection do not recommend it, but the fact is that users almost invariably use the same password for all the sensitive documents they create. Thus, once the word is discovered, all of that user's files can be accessed.

The other drawback, as one senior user recently said, is that if a secretary were knocked down and killed and there was no means of circumventing the procedure, accessing her files would be impossible and they would die with her. There is a means by which this can be achieved although it requires skills not normally present in most users and is not widely known.

The 'erase' facility is a vulnerable one which should be protected against misuse by a disgruntled employee or an intruder by ensuring that the power source to the equipment is capable of being locked off when not in authorised use.

Calculations can be made on a word processor by means of a mathematics support package. This additional software is used for calculations which have to be done frequently, such as those used to assess yields from investments. The calculation is stored on disc; the user merely inserts the variable data, and the machine tells him whether the investment is worthwhile or not. For example, an oil company contemplating purchasing a garage site could calculate the return on investment using a formula already set up on the processor; they would simply insert the proposed capital outlay, the cost of re-equipping, and the projected income from sales and services to discover whether the site was worthy of investment.

Since the multipliers and dividers set up will be utilised but not 'seen', the danger is that deliberate alteration of one of the factors could make a disastrous investment look very promising. Timely substitution of the proper program for other, similar calculations could mask the irregularity and if the variation achieved is not so obvious that a quick check of 'reasonableness' would reveal it, the spurious program could well go undetected.

12 Using Outside Resources

Security has come a long way in the last two decades. Gone is the old night watchman crouched over his brazier throughout the silent hours. In his place a range of specialists from the traditional uniformed guard, trained in physical security and access control, to the qualified practitioner skilled in risk management, loss prevention and industrial counter-espionage.

Individuals skilled in counter-espionage may well come from the military or the security services, adapting the skills learned there to the requirements of commerce and industry. There are no formal qualifications in the speciality but the expertise and techniques still have to be acquired and familiarisation gained with the type of equipment available on the market.

Effective counter measures depend on knowledge of offensive techniques. Therefore, competence has to be gained by experimenting with different types of offensive devices in a variety of situations. So wide is the range of offensive techniques and equipment that the cost of training anyone in the techniques of industrial counter-espionage may be a limiting factor; as may the need to ensure that those 'experimenting' with offensive devices are not at risk of prosecution for 'using' them. The only safe solution would seem to be the training courses run by manufacturers of countering equipment in countries where such activities are lawful.

Even after training, in the operational techniques, of electronic sweeping say, the specialist will need, as a minimum, a piece of equipment costing around £18.000.

The high costs mean there will always be the
temptation to subcontract this type of security function,
on the grounds that the skills are too specialised and
would not be required frequently enough to justify
in-house specialists. To employ them would require a
substantial outlay of capital and any return on investment would be difficult to project.

Contracted security v in-house security

There may be apparent advantages in using contracted
security such as reducing the payroll, avoiding over-
heads on employees and the expense of training. One
very real advantage is that you can require the
contractor to remove any person who does not suit you.

But these should be weighed against the major
disadvantage, the split loyalties that divide all contracted employees. For uniformed guards working to
clearly defined instructions the risk may be acceptable.
The case for employing contracted rather than in-house
personnel has perhaps been proved in this area.
Indeed, Scotland Yard employs contracted security
guards to vet all visitors, thus releasing the police
officers who used to carry out this function for more
important duties.

It is unwise, however, to employ contracted security
specialists for functions as sensitive as industrial
counter-espionage. Apart from the high fees charged
for electronic sweeping, it is an area which attracts
self-appointed specialists, skilled only in the art of
electronic deception: the art of impressing or confusing
clients with powerful-looking gadgets that emit electronic sounds, show flickering lights or create traces on a
visual display unit, but do virtually nothing.

There are, of course, many technically competent

specialists who use good and effective equipment that is capable of detecting both dead and live bugs. But even here the pressure to produce results may cause problems. Take the case of one such specialist who, having 'swept' the boardroom of a major company for several months, feared that, since he had found nothing, his services would be dispensed with and suddenly 'found' a bug. He had in fact taken it to the premises with him and produced it like a magician pulling a rabbit from a top hat!

This sort of thing highlights the inadvisability of using an outside agency for such work. There are not only pressures on client and specialist alike to produce results, culminating in the sort of deception just described, but a client exposes that vital factor, the integrity of his boardroom, to a complete stranger, jeopardising all his planning and expenditure in providing outer layers of security.

It is not unknown for specialists to seek to infiltrate a target company by offering a protective service and then, under the guise of searching for hidden devices, plant one!

The more desperate and less honourable practitioner may, as a matter of course, always leave a recording device, speculating that any information gleaned must be of some value to someone somewhere!

Security specialists are unlikely to offer actual offensive services, but if business is bad and financial problems imminent, very little persuasion is required for the person or firm set up to provide a defensive service to engage in an offensive one for the right price.

The argument in favour of using one's own security personnel, trained specifically for the task and armed with effective detection equipment, is formidable, particularly if the equipment used offers a money-back guarantee if it is not successful in detecting a device in the first 60 days.

As an additional safeguard, two operatives should be trained and fully conversant with the equipment. Not only does this cover absences, it reflects the principle that security is always enhanced if two or more persons are involved in a highly critical function.

13   *Conclusions*

Just as the police cannot alone prevent crime but need the co-operation and assistance of the public, security in an organisation cannot prevent crimes and acts of industrial espionage without the commitment and support of the employees in whose interests the various systems have been devised or instituted. Crime prevention is a matter for everyone, not simply those members of staff whose particular responsibility it is.

Prevention is always better than cure. It is also usually less expensive and certainly less disruptive or traumatic. It is the difference between predetermined and controlled response and hastily devised reaction.

A recent survey in the USA estimates that over 10,000 illegal bugs are planted each year — more than 20 times the frequency of legal law enforcement bugging. Since this is only one means of improperly obtaining confidential information, the total number of offences using all means must be staggering! Add to this the fact that most incidents of this nature are never detected, and those that are, are suppressed from public knowledge — large companies fearing losses on the stock market following such embarrassing publicity — and the dimensions of the problem must give any employer cause for grave concern. No one can afford to be complacent about it.

Appendix:
An Anton Piller Order

Upon the Plaintiff's undertaking to abide by any Order this Court may make as to damages in case this Court shall hereafter be of the opinion that the Defendants shall have sustained any loss by reason of this Order which the Plaintiffs ought to pay;

It is Ordered that: –

1. The Defendants whether by themselves, their servants or agents or any of them or otherwise howsoever shall permit such persons not exceeding 3 as may be duly authorised by the Plaintiffs and members or employees not exceeding 2 of the Plaintiffs' solicitors forthwith to enter the premises known as (address) or such parts thereof as shall be occupied or used by the Defendants at any hour between 8 o'clock in the forenoon and 6 o'clock in the evening of (date) for the purpose of (a) inspecting and photographing (description of documents and property in question) and (b) removing (such property as belongs to the Plaintiffs or is evidence of the matters in question in the action).

2. The Defendants be restrained and an injunction is granted restraining them whether by themselves, their servants or agents or otherwise howsoever from in any way altering defacing or destroying or removing from the premises any of (the articles documents or property) referred to in paragraph 1 without leave of the Court.

And it is further ordered that:—

The Defendants do forthwith by their servants or agents AB and CD disclose to the person who shall serve this Order upon them the names and addresses of all persons firms or companies known to them:

    i) to whom or to which the Defendants or one or more of them have supplied or offered to supply illicit copy films with the quantities and dates thereof.

    ii) who have supplied or offered to supply the Defendants or one or more of them with illicit copy films with the quantities and dates thereof, and

    iii) who are engaged in the production distribution offer for sale or sale of illicit copy films

and the said Defendants do within 4 days after service upon them of this Order make and serve upon the Plaintiffs' solicitors an affidavit setting forth the information which they are required to give pursuant to the foregoing part of this Order and exhibiting thereto all invoices labels books of account letters lists and other documents within their respective possession power custody or control which relate to each and every illicit film (or whatever) supplied or offered by or to the Defendants.

Index

The Author

After service in the Admiralty and the Royal Navy, **Michael Saunders** worked as an Investigations Officer in the British Customs and Excise Force for thirteen years before moving into industrial security as an investigator for a large oil company. For the last five years Mr Saunders has been an independent security consultant, and in this capacity his work has included regularly appearing in court as an expert witness on intruder alarm systems and investigating marine frauds for the International Maritime Bureau. He is a member of the (UK) Institute of Industrial Security, the International Professional Security Association and the American Society for Industrial Security, and an instructor on the advanced fraud course at the Metropolitan Police College. He has written numerous articles on security and is co-author of a book *Hi-Tech Homes*.